REPUBLICANS
AND
VIETNAM

Recent Titles in
Contributions in Political Science
Series Editor: Bernard K. Johnpoll

With Dignity: The Search for Medicare and Medicaid
Sheri I. David

American Prince, American Pauper: The Contemporary Vice-Presidency in Perspective
Marie D. Natoli

Shadow Justice: The Ideology and Institutionalization of Alternatives to Court
Christine B. Harrington

Daniel Bell and the Agony of Modern Liberalism
Nathan Liebowitz

The Flacks of Washington: Government Information and the Public Agenda
David R. Morgan

Workers, Participation, and Democracy: Internal Politics in the British Union Movement
Joel D. Wolfe

A Political Organization Approach to Transnational Terrorism
Kent Layne Oots

Individualism and Community: The State in Marx and Early Anarchism
Jeffrey H. Barker

Sentinels of Empire: The United States and Latin American Militarism
Jan Knippers Black

Portugal in the 1980's: Dilemmas of Democratic Consolidation
Kenneth Maxwell, editor

Dependency Theory and the Return of High Politics
Mary Ann Tetreault and Charles Frederick Abel, editors

Ban the Bomb: A History of SANE, the Committee for a Sane Nuclear Policy, 1957–1985
Milton S. Katz

REPUBLICANS AND VIETNAM, 1961–1968

Terry Dietz

CONTRIBUTIONS IN POLITICAL SCIENCE, NUMBER 146

GREENWOOD PRESS
NEW YORK • WESTPORT, CONNECTICUT • LONDON

Library of Congress Cataloguing-in-Publication Data

Dietz, Terry.
  Republicans and Vietnam, 1961–1968.

  (Contributions in political science, ISSN 0147–1066 ;
no. 146)
  Bibliography: p.
  Includes index.
  1. Vietnamese Conflict, 1961–1975—United States.
2. United States—Politics and government—1961–1963.
3. United States—Politics and government—1965–1969.
4. Republican Party (U.S. : 1854–   ) I. Title.
II. Series
DS558.D54 1986   959.704′33′73   85–24764
ISBN 0–313–24892–3 (lib. bdg. : alk. paper)

Library of Congress Catalog Card Number: 85–24764
ISBN: 0–313–24892–3
ISSN: 0147–1066

First published in 1986

Greenwood Press, Inc.
88 Post Road West
Westport, Connecticut 06881

Printed in the United States of America

The paper used in this book complies with the
Permanent Paper Standard issued by the National
Information Standards Organization (Z39.48–1984).

10 9 8 7 6 5 4 3 2 1

To the memory of
my grandparents
Charles A. and Jeanette Young

CONTENTS

Illustrations   ix

Preface   xi

1. The Mantle of World Leadership   1

2. The Ev and Charlie Show vs. JFK   33

3. The Grand Old Party Divided   57

4. The Oil Can and the Sword   95

5. A Legacy of Transition   143

   Notes   157

   Bibliography   173

   Index   179

ILLUSTRATIONS

Following page 56:

1. Senator Arthur Vandenberg, 1948

2. Senator Robert Taft

3. President John F. Kennedy with Democratic and Republican leaders at baseball season opener, 1963

4. Republican Leadership Breakfast, 1965

5. Senator Everett Dirksen with President Lyndon Johnson, 1964

6. The "Ev and Jerry Show," 1966

7. House Minority Leader Gerald Ford delivers Republican State of the Union message, 1967

8. Republican leaders, 1968

9. Ford and Dirksen with President Johnson, 1968

PREFACE

The work and research for this book began in earnest during 1981 after some very serious reflections on my part about the Republican response to the Vietnam War. I was fascinated by the interrelationship between foreign policy, war policy, and politics. Initially, I investigated how the congressional leadership responded to America's role in Vietnam, but eventually expanded the scope to include key leaders within the Republican Party. As the title of this book notes, the time frame for this volume runs from 1961 to 1968. This was a period when Republicans were the party out of power on the national level and sought to perform their role as the loyal opposition within the federal government. Therefore, this book is not an overall history of the Vietnam War but a study of opposition politics as John F. Kennedy and Lyndon B. Johnson held the White House and their party controlled Congress.

"Loyal opposition" is a term rooted in the Anglo–American legislative system which designates that the party out of power oppose those in control of the political system. The concept of a loyal opposition has been divided traditionally into two categories: the first requires that the opposition question, amend, or offer alternatives to those positions advocated by the majority, including the president; the second, which is the underpinning of our democracy, requires loyalty. It is not a loyalty based on blind faith in one individual or program but a belief that the system in and of itself is worthwhile and should be preserved beyond simple partisan gain. Consequently, the minority does not seek to destroy the governmental structure but promotes changes within a constitutional framework.

The Republican party performed its role as the loyal opposition during the time period prior to and after World War II, during the Korean War, and in the 1960s during the Vietnam War. It was, however, during the 1960s that Republicans, and the American people as a whole, faced one of the severest tests in the nation's history. Ironically, the Grand Old Party (GOP) supported America's commitment to help South Vietnam remain free, but Republicans had no direct control over war policy, which led to a curious and frustrating set of circumstances. How could the minority party challenge Lyndon Johnson's prosecution of the war, not undermine America's international standing, protect the men in the field, and still perform its role as the loyal opposition? The answers were far from simple, and the dilemmas faced by Republican leaders taxed the best of statesmen.

It should be noted that Republicans have come a long way since the isolationist days of the 1930s prior to World War II. After 1945 it was statesmen such as Michigan's Senator Arthur Vandenberg who advocated bipartisanship as a way to stop politics at the water's edge. Bipartisanship sought to replace the traditional political division on foreign affairs during the early years after World War II. Democrats and Republicans sought some form of common ground when America's foreign policy interests were at stake, and this was a key component of Vandenberg's concept. But the Republican direction of foreign policy was limited. Except for Dwight D. Eisenhower's two terms as president in the 1950s, the GOP never held control of the White House between 1933 and 1968. Its control over the Congress during the same time period was even more limited.

The conflict in Southeast Asia divided America more than any single event since the Civil War. During the Vietnam War, Republicans first supported Kennedy's policies and then Johnson's aims in Vietnam. The recurring irony, though, was that Republicans criticized Johnson's tactics and methods of warfare but never changed the outcome of the conflict. Republicans, especially congressional leaders, sought some sort of input on Vietnam and the ensuing U.S. military role. Everett Dirksen, Charles Halleck, and Gerald Ford personified the leadership reaction from Congress, while Richard Nixon, Barry Goldwater, George Romney, and Nelson Rockefeller helped orchestrate the party response.

My goals during the researching and writing of this book were to explain briefly the Republican philosophy on foreign affairs in the years shortly after 1945, the Republican view on Vietnam and how Republican feelings were made known, and the internal policy-making procedures that the loyal opposition employed as it fulfilled its crucial function of criticizing the Democrats in power between 1961 and 1968. Republicans were usually quite willing to attack President Kennedy and later President Johnson for their domestic policies and programs. The latter, especially, faced severe criticism on the social programs and services contained in the Great Society legislation. But when it came to foreign policy and Vietnam, Republicans desired basic national unity. The question arises, could the Vietnam War have ended on a different note had GOP leaders, especially from Congress, been heeded? It is an issue open to debate, and it is my hope that this book raises some very serious questions about the minority party's role on the national level and the future direction of America's foreign policy.

Since this book covers a set topic and time frame, it was necessary to select key primary and secondary sources, as well as policy-makers, that would add commentary about the war and the political response to it. In order to understand the decision-making process during the Kennedy and Johnson administrations, several standard works were chosen and digested so the reader might fully comprehend how and why policy developed and the path that policy eventually followed. It also was necessary to rely upon Republican party documents as a source for some of the philosophical directions in which the GOP was moving or that it eventually chose. In other instances, the public record from statements by Republican leaders in the *New York Times* gives the reader a sense of where the party was going.

My sincere desire was to represent as many segments of the Republican party as possible. Unfortunately, numerous individuals could not, or would not, grant me interviews concerning my research. After making a good-faith effort, the following were still unavailable: Senators Barry Goldwater, Howard Baker, Thomas Kuchel, Edward Brooke, Mark Hatfield, Richard Lugar, Charles Percy, and Jacob Javits. Others included former President Richard

Nixon, Justice Richard Poff, and Mr. John Rhodes. I was able to speak with a number of leaders, however, who conveyed the inner workings of policy formulation during the 1960s.

John Donne once wrote that "no man is an island," and this was so blatantly true as I labored over the manuscript. This work would never have been completed without the help of many people. I am indebted to Meredith Berg from Valparaiso University, who consistently advised me on this topic, read several drafts through the years, and offered criticism on the thematic development. Leland Thornton from Glen Oaks Community College consulted with me on numerous issues and helped place many salient points in perspective. The late William Downard from St. Joseph's College provided crucial guidance. Bill was not only one of my former professors but also a friend who shared his expertise by doing several manuscript critiques through the years. I am especially thankful that he knew, shortly before his death, that this book was nearing its conclusion. His wise counsel will be deeply missed in the future. Among the others who read various drafts, or sections, and provided me with insight were Glenn and Dorys Sperandio, Anne Alstott, Bruce Johnson, Bill Fraser, Mark Speedy, Janie Norman, Bob St. Clair, and Ken Schmid, Jr. Renée Cannock also deserves a word of thanks for her proficient typing of the final draft.

To those individuals who granted me personal interviews, I am deeply indebted; without their help this book would have been nearly impossible to complete. In some cases they were reluctant to discuss the sensitive issue of Vietnam, but each one provided me with valuable information. There were instances when these people wished to be off the record, and I have endeavored to keep those conversations that way. President Gerald Ford allowed me two interviews so that I might fully understand the topics and issues at hand. Among the others in the political realm who gave me access were Senators J. William Fulbright, Hugh Scott, John Tower, Charles Goodell, John Sherman Cooper, Judge Jack Miller from the United States Court of Appeals in Washington, former Congressmen Melvin Laird, Bob Wilson, and Charles Halleck. Former New York City Mayor John Lindsay, Governor George Romney, Dr. William Prendergast, Mr. McGeorge Bundy, Mr. Bill Baroody, Mr. Seth Tilman, Mr. Pat Holt, and Mr. Cran Montgomery also gave time for interviews. Vice President George Bush answered written questions. Among others who assisted me in the political area were Father D. F. Shea, formerly of the Republican National Committee, Mr. Wes Bucher of the Indiana Republican State Committee, Senator Dan Quayle, and Congressman G. William Whitehurst and staff. Congressman John Myers and his staff also aided me in so many ways that I cannot even begin to list them on paper.

Libraries hold copious amounts of knowledge, but good research librarians are essential in retrieving such material. My special thanks goes to Helen Schroyer of Purdue University who not only read one of my drafts but was immensely helpful in providing pertinent material during the years of research and writing. The staff of the Lyndon B. Johnson Library was extremely kind, and I am grateful for assistance from Claudia Anderson and Linda Hanson; the latter especially tolerated my incessant questions and requests. Barbara Anderson and the staff of the John F. Kennedy Library were gracious with their help, as was Janet Lange from the Everett Dirksen Congressional Research Center at Pekin, Illinois.

One of the greatest advantages afforded me as an educator through the years has been the many wonderful students who have been in my American government classes. I was even more fortunate in that two of these former students aided me as research assistants. Steve Riggs not only served as my Washington liaison but also conducted extensive research on my behalf on numerous occasions and read several drafts of the manuscript. Steve's understanding of the political process in Washington helped pave the way for some crucial interviews. He accompanied me when I met Judge Jack Miller, Dr. William Prendergast, Senator Charles Goodell, and Senator John Tower. Steve's commitment and contributions were exceptional, and I am very grateful for his assistance. The second person is Mike Bates. He read several drafts of this book, conducted research, and accompanied me to the LBJ Library. He also aided me as I prepared for several interviews. Mike always tried to help, no matter what the problem happened to be, and his genuine enthusiasm lightened my load more than he will ever know. Finally, I must thank Bill, Mark, Bruce, Janie, and Susie for always being there when I needed them.

REPUBLICANS
AND
VIETNAM

1.

THE MANTLE OF WORLD LEADERSHIP

Politics is a dynamic process. No finer illustration of this fact is the American political system. The bending, shaping, and molding of our nation is both visible and hidden. Another factor of consequence for politics is history and the movement inherent with change. For the United States the elements of politics and history have intermingled to alter the very destiny of this nation, and in several cases, the world. Some political policy decisions are easy to see, simple to gauge. Others, however, are made behind the scenes without ever being open to view by the electorate. But policy decisions in and of themselves are not created in a vacuum; they are subject to problems and events from overseas, which may be historical in nature but have a momentum of their own. There is a point in time when politics and history meet, forcing the nation towards a different course. Inevitably the question will arise, who and what determines this new course? It is hoped that leaders will make the right choices, but one must remember that they are products of their time and history. What influences American leaders to act the way they do can usually be determined by examining the past and understanding the difficult actions that must be taken when a situation beckons a choice.

Within our governmental system the Republican party, as well as the United States, faced a new role in world leadership in the fateful year of 1945. The stakes grew even larger during the 1960s as American power and prestige were tied to a nation in Southeast Asia called Vietnam. Here too the Republicans played a role. As a minority party within our national government, the Grand Old

Party (GOP) had to play second chair in a drama that profoundly affected the spirit and direction of our nation. Even in its limited role, GOP weight was felt throughout the political process. World War II and the Korean War had given the party practice for the minority position. Vietnam was more than just a simple matter of frustration and anxiety for Republicans; it was a conflict which altered our politics drastically and established new historical lessons for the future. In one sense, Republicans helped direct the American policy towards Vietnam; in another, they were caught in the whirlwind of Vietnam and reacted to it.

From the historical standpoint, the Republican party has been linked with what historian George Mayer called "a virile nationalism in foreign affairs, although there was persistent disagreement as to the desirability of entanglement abroad in peacetime."[1] Defining the national interest, in terms of foreign affairs, had always been a debatable topic. Precise formulas offered little, if any, guidance. As Americans surveyed the scene at the turn of the century, they found other nations playing power politics. At the very least, this was a despicable game which required an aloof attitude on behalf of our nation. Hans Morgenthau has observed that our role as a spectator was relished during the 1800s. We could watch the world race by and observe the political game or rely on the belief that eventually democracy would be established everywhere, and "the final curtain would fall and the game of power politics would no longer be played."[2] By the early 1900s, though, Republicans on the national level had formulated fundamental beliefs on American participation within the international community.

Senator Hugh Scott, a Republican from Pennsylvania, has argued that westward expansion, a free market economy at the turn of the century, and the internationalist sympathies of a William McKinley and Theodore Roosevelt allowed for a Pacific orientation within the Republican party. Through acquisition of Hawaii and the Philippines the belief in manifest destiny was carried further west. Scott has also theorized that the Democratic preoccupation towards Europe may lie in the political makeup of the Democratic party with European immigrants coming through Ellis Island and centering in the urban East. Consequently, the party has a strong European heritage.[3]

More recently—from the 1940s on—Republicans have found themselves divided between two camps: (1) an international wing, most prominently led by Dwight Eisenhower or Nelson Rockefeller and (2) an isolationist, or non-interventionist, wing—usually associated with Senator Robert Taft. Keeping these positions in mind, noted diplomatic historian Thomas Bailey has observed, "[c]onservative Republicans have been more favorable to intervening against Communism in Asia ('Asia Firsters') than in Europe."[4] In part, Bailey's observation may help to explain why the GOP was more willing to support fighting in Vietnam. The problem once again has been to define the national interest. Sometimes a Barry Goldwater and an Eisenhower may have been in agreement over foreign affairs. Hence, the lines are not always clear cut and there may be a great deal of overlapping in terms of positions. No matter which stance Republican politicians took—involvement or isolation—the watershed for the direction of American foreign policy was World War II.

The American position prior to World War II, and even World War I, had been an uneasiness with foreign affairs. As a nation, we never felt aligned with the European system or its power politics. Norman Graebner, in his book *Cold War Diplomacy: American Foreign Policy 1945–1960*, makes a distinct observation about the American perspective. Between 1900 and 1945 we were a satisfied power and not prone to seeking territorial gains. In short, we had an interest in stability. This satisfaction was coupled with our need to seek morality within the context of international relationships. Americans have never really viewed war as part of the traditional ebb and flow for the world's political system; consequently, our perspective on foreign affairs was extremely self-limiting.

World War II, and the ensuing peace, forced us into an unfamiliar situation by 1945. That posture was quite simple: at the war's end we were the strongest political, economic, and military power in the world. Yet we had little control, if any, over other nations such as the Soviet Union. In other words, our power had limits. A new situation, by necessity, forced a change in American thinking over international relations. We no longer had the luxury of remaining isolated from the world order, and the reason for this centered on a change in the balance of power. Europe was in a shambles, a power vacuum also had been created in the Far East and Asia when Japan was defeated, and the United States faced the Soviet Union which seemed determined to expand its influence and borders.[5]

When the Potsdam Conference convened in Germany in July 1945, the world political situation had assumed an air of bipolarity. The Soviets were unwilling to compromise on the question of a free Eastern Europe, nor had we developed adequate policies for dealing with the Soviets. On one hand, Americans espoused principles of "free elections" and "self-determination" for the peoples of occupied Europe. The other hand was busy cutting the number of men in uniform. President Harry Truman was responding to pressure from Congress and the public to "bring the boys home" and demilitarize. As we now look back, some nations may have read this move as an unwillingness to back up our word with force. One should understand, however, that our position was not necessarily one of weakness. We did possess an atomic capability and would strive to develop that power in the postwar period to a nuclear superiority. Our economic and industrial base, as well as the political and social institutions, were intact, thereby allowing Americans a cohesive structure that would enable them to meet fundamental Soviet challenges.

This new bipolar world had been created from conflict within the old order of nations. Psychologically and diplomatically the pressure was upon the United States to adapt, change, and cope with the new order. The traditional forces that once had restrained the Soviet Union were now gone. This degeneration of restraint began in World War I with the defeat of Austria and Turkey, which had helped to keep Czarist Russia within its boundaries. Further erosion of the wall against Soviet expansion took place when England and France declined as major international powers. After two world wars, Anglo-French strength slipped to its lowest ebb in centuries; therefore, restraints upon the Soviet Union were minimal at best by 1945.

By May 1945 the second major conflict of this century on Europe's fields was ending. Germany lay in ruins and there was no Continental power strong enough to meet the Soviets with comparative strength. But the disintegration of European power started prior to 1945. One could argue that the fall of Czechoslovakia and Poland in the 1930s sounded the death knell for a balance of power within Europe, and this extremely unsettling situation faced America's new leader, Harry Truman, as world conflict concluded.

Franklin Roosevelt's death in April 1945 forced Truman into a presidency that would encounter profound decisions and problems in the postwar period. At this time in our political history, the Republicans were in the minority on Capitol Hill, but even this did not dissuade them from adopting a tough stance towards the Soviet Union. They became the primary movers with a "hardline" approach in dealing with Moscow. As Graebner has noted:

Congressional Republicans had supported Roosevelt's wartime policies and decisions. But by the autumn of 1945 it was quite obvious that the wartime effort had brought the nation far less security and peace than the President had promised or that the American expenditures had warranted. Republicans now demanded of Truman what Roosevelt had failed to achieve: a world of justice built on the Atlantic Charter.[6]

All of these challenges were unsettling for Americans as a whole, and new strategies were necessary so that the Soviet Union could be dealt with as a major force. Our wartime alliance with the Soviets had been shaky at best, because there was a mutual distrust. In reality, though, the arrangement was a matter of convenience against a common enemy. Roosevelt's vision of a "grand alliance" never really materialized; therefore, postwar cooperation was exceedingly limited.

A member of the State Department, George Kennan, formulated a theory in the late 1940s on how the Soviets were to be halted in their expansion over other nations. Kennan had been with the foreign service in several diplomatic posts overseas; his major contribution, though, was development of the containment policy. Essentially, Kennan argued that American responses to Soviet moves had to be structured in such a way as to meet challenges wherever and whenever they appeared. The new policy included economic or military aid and, if necessary, troops. But the goal was fairly well defined—contain communism within its borders. Containment faced several tests between 1945 and 1950, the most notable being in Greece and Turkey during the late 1940s. However, as mentioned earlier, the idea of containing the Russian empire was not necessarily original. In fact, one prominent United States senator has argued that containment was just a replacement for the "egg and spoon" idea which England practiced for years. According to Senator John Tower of Texas, "Russia was seen as the egg and that what surrounded it [England] was the spoon." When British power could no longer force "containment of czarist imperialism," we inherited the policy. Therefore, we were assuming a policy that was not necessarily unique in world politics but was new from the American perspective of global participation. Whatever its name, the United States was in a different international role and its main opponent was the Soviet Union.[7]

Changes in the balance of power were understood by Truman and in most cases by his political opposition in the Republican party. Since 1933, the GOP had chafed under the position as a minority party playing second fiddle to the New Deal and Franklin Roosevelt. A general theme running through Republican thought prior to Pearl Harbor was a belief in noninvolvement overseas or what some prefer to label as isolationism. Semantics aside, the bombing of Pearl Harbor on December 7, 1941 was a decisive turning point for Republican philosophy. An individual who personified this profound change was Arthur Vandenberg.

As a Republican senator from Michigan, Vandenberg represented his state in Washington from 1928 until his death in 1951. He had been involved with Michigan's Republican State Central Committee as well as being a reporter, editor, and eventually general manager of a Grand Rapids newspaper. He was appointed to the United States Senate in 1928 to fill a vacancy created by the death of another senator. He subsequently was reelected for three consecutive terms.

During the early stage of his public career, Vandenberg was an ardent isolationist and did not believe in profound American involvement overseas. In 1937 he co-authored a resolution which sought to take the profit out of material production for war, and he also helped author a neutrality act in the 1930s designed to keep America out of conflict, or possible conflict, in Europe. Much of the reaction to war profiteering was a direct result of charges stemming from World War I and directed towards those who made fortunes from the sale of war materials. Without question, he was one of the leading isolationists within the nation prior to World War II.

Vandenberg, however, holds an unusual place within modern American history because his conversion to an internationalist stance illustrated a major personal turning point as well as the watershed for the Republican party during the 1940s. He wrote, "[M]y convictions regarding international cooperation and security for peace took firm form on the afternoon of the Pearl Harbor attack. That day ended isolationism for any realist."[8] Later, his work at the San Francisco Conference in 1945—which helped establish the United Nations—and his efforts to secure the Senate ratification of the United Nations Charter helped strengthen the American position overseas. But his influence did not cease after these goals were reached. Vandenberg achieved even further recognition with his formulation and advocacy of bipartisanship—a policy which sought some form of domestic unity over the American role in foreign affairs.

A major cornerstone of Republican bipartisanship during the 1940s and 1950s was the Michigan senator's tradition of unity at the "water's edge." His definition and conditions were as follows:

Bipartisan foreign policy is not the result of political coercion but of nonpolitical conviction. I never have even pretended to speak for my party in foreign policy activities. I have relied upon the validity of my actions to command whatever support they may deserve. I have never made any semblance of a partisan demand for support and I never shall. . . . I expect every Republican, like every Democrat, to respond to his own conscience. I expect them all to yield their judgments, at such an hour, to the political dictates of any party managers. On the latter basis, bipartisan foreign policy would die in revolt. I hope we may avoid that tragedy.[9]

Obviously, this definition ranks high in idealism, which subjects it to severe tests in circumstances other than war. His goal, however, was domestic unity whenever possible in relation to our global role. In an idealistic and yet practical way, Vandenberg saw genuine purpose in bipartisanship. The senator, in a book edited by his son, outlined the advantages:

The purpose of this unity is to strengthen American security and sustain American ideals by giving maximum authority to America's voice for peace with justice. In the face of a foreign problem, our unity is as important as a discouragement to alien miscalculation which, otherwise, might lead to the mistaken belief that we are vulnerable because of our domestic divisions. It is our best available insurance for peace.[10]

Although the actual definition of bipartisanship quoted here was not completely formed until after World War II, Roosevelt and Truman realized that Republicans had to be part of the decision-making process at the war's end. Roosevelt, especially, did not want to repeat Woodrow Wilson's error of 1919 when he failed to bring key Republicans into consultation during the Versailles Peace Conference which ended World War I. The lessons of history demanded that new tactics be adopted by both the president and the opposition party within the Congress, in this case the Republicans. This new situation forced the minority party to reconsider its role.

Traditionally, in American history the party out of power is required to question the policies of those in political power and in some cases offer alternatives. This concept is known as the loyal opposition within the American system and can be traced back to British history and the minority role within Parliament. Even though one party is out of power, it is their duty to oppose the group in control while remaining loyal to the governmental system. Republicans faced this role three times in recent history: during and after World War II, during the Korean War, and during the 1960s with Vietnam. But by the late 1940s a number of people questioned Vandenberg's stance as a Republican supporting a Democrat (Roosevelt and Truman) administration. (Most politicians, though, will make a distinction on the role of a loyal opposition. A vigorous fight should be made on domestic issues, but with situations overseas other nations should not be allowed to divide the parties.)

Vandenberg and his Republican predecessors faced the serious problem of how to retain their political independence, develop constructive alternatives, and yet not appear as unpatriotic. This required a delicate balancing act surrounded by perilous alternatives. It is crucial to understand that Arthur Vandenberg's conversion to internationalism paved the way for some sort of Republican input during the postwar period. In fact, he may have been crucial to the success of Truman's programs abroad, but the Michigan senator was quick to point out that he was neither a "Co-Secretary of State" nor some foreign policy wizard. Vandenberg understood that consultation between the president and members of the Republican party was essential if policies were to succeed. What had to be determined was which policy served the national interest, how was it to be implemented, and then determine whether or not it was successful. He still realized that there would be political differences, but through mutual consultation he believed strong partisan rancor could be avoided.

A major complaint that Vandenberg had with presidents was the "crisis method" of diplomacy. Typically, there would be a summons to the White House, and reports of dire consequences would be given with a plea for concerted action among the political forces within Washington. Instead, he thought some sort of continuous policy development was desirable. American politics being the way it is, and was in the 1940s, usually has left little room for bipartisanship; therefore problems are inherent with this political form. Critics of bipartisanship have charged that Vandenberg surrendered his position as a key Republican leader, but he was wise enough to see that changes in the world order demanded internal political changes for the United States. His vision of bipartisanship was limited, though, to the creation of the United Nations and to Europe. Palestine (now Israel) and China were excluded from this vision; he felt that bipartisanship would not work everywhere.[11]

Bipartisanship aside, Vandenberg was not the only senator to exercise influence over foreign affairs. In fact, Republicans had reorganized themselves within the congressional structure, and this new form spread key positions among several members. The genesis for this reform was the Legislative Reorganization Act of 1946, which went into effect during 1947. Development of a Republican Policy Committee and the Republican Conference were designed to give members more input with relation to new proposals or policies. These groups also served as an information tool for the party leaders; they could spread new ideas as well as poll their member's feelings on key issues. When these groups were combined with the traditional floor leader's role, they served to provide a three-pronged approach. What you had in effect were a chairman of the conference, chairman of the policy committee, and the minority leader in each chamber helping to establish Republican policy in Congress. As we shall see, this reorganization provided a limited form of unity for Republican philosophy, but the real test of this organization came during the 1960s when House and Senate members questioned the American role in Vietnam. During the late 1940s, though, this new hierarchy served to unify congressional members of the GOP. Malcolm Jewell, an astute observer of the legislative branch and especially the Senate, has written: "Lacking the President as a unifying force, the opposition party is likely to be divided on foreign policy, but it must constantly seek unity if it is to influence the administration's policy or even establish a record for itself."[12] The policy committee tried to do just that—help establish Republican policy; the conference was designed to keep all Republicans united and provide a platform for them to express their individual thoughts; and the floor leader's position allowed a key member of the party to steer Republican business through the congressional maze.

During the early postwar period, Vandenberg had been a prime mover in the Republican foreign policy circles. His expertise was an acknowledged fact, but he shared power in the Senate with another member of his own party, Robert Taft of Ohio.

Ohio has produced politicians of national prominence, but one of its most famous was Robert A. Taft. Son of the former president and chief justice of the United States, William Howard Taft, Robert Taft served in the Ohio legislature before winning a U.S. Senate campaign in 1938. He continued as a member of the Senate until his death in July 1953.

Taft was viewed by many as "Mr. Republican" because of his impeccable educational credentials and his championing of the midwestern conservative-isolationist wing of the Republican party. An attorney by vocation, he graduated first in his class from Yale and was first in his class upon graduation from Harvard Law School. Prior to World War II he was an isolationist, but he never converted to internationalism in the fashion of Vandenberg; rather, he opposed Truman's concentration on Europe during the postwar period and argued that Asia merited more American attention. During the reorganization of 1947 he chaired the Republican Policy Committee and held that position until he died. His influence became more pronounced when he was elected the majority leader in the Senate during the latter part of 1952. Republicans had wrested control of the Congress from the Democratic party for the second time in twenty years, and Taft was one of the key leaders in the Senate during the early 1950s.

Therefore, Republicans had two key senators, each from the Midwest, and each believing that certain areas of the globe were more crucial than others. In a sense, Vandenberg had achieved his input with Europe, but Taft was to lead a fight against Truman and Korea. Vandenberg had been a senior member of the Senate Foreign Relations Committee, but as was noted earlier Taft chaired the policy committee.[13]

Leadership positions are useful, of course, but the important factor lies in the person who occupies the position. The power is still fragmented and the inherent skill that a person possesses determines his influence. This is where political judgment enters, because it separates leaders from followers. But judgment is composed of more than political savvy. On the contrary, it demands intelligence, insight, perception, and in many cases luck. As we have seen, Vandenberg played a major role in the postwar world and used his political skill and expertise to champion bipartisanship. However, the very nature of the legislative system also determines the extent to which members of Congress may respond to foreign affairs.

The House of Representatives makes it difficult for someone to aspire to the position of a statesman. A two-year term, the size of the chamber, and the small size of a congressional district closer to the people prohibit direct influence over foreign affairs. But this was the original intent of the Founding Fathers. The Senate is more removed from the role of direct representation. A six-year term allows senators to survey a situation with a greater degree of objectivity. The Constitution also bestows upon the Senate a power called "advice and consent," which applies to treaties, appointments, and, eventually, foreign affairs. It is understandable that the Senate's role increased in importance during World War II and the late 1940s.[14]

At the beginning of the postwar period, the primary objectives of American foreign policy were directed towards Europe, since the menace of Communist expansion seemed to pose the largest threat. Another area of concern was the Far East, and Japan's defeat created a second power vacuum whose impact was to be felt on the Asian continent.

According to Allied plans during World War II, mainland China was to play a major role in international affairs once conflict ceased.

China was to have a seat on the United Nations Security Council, become a major power in the Pacific, and serve as a countervailing force to the Soviets in the region. The Chinese failed to meet all of these high expectations, because internal political and economic strife plagued the nation before, during, and after the war. China had experimented with democracy during the 1920s, but its lack of cohesiveness, essential to the democratic tradition, was absent.

Chiang Kai-shek, leader of the Nationalist Chinese forces and pro-American, was unable to control all areas of his nation. The antagonist to Chiang's rule and eventual winner in the Chinese Civil War was Mao Tse-tung, who led the Communist forces. Prior to the Japanese invasion in the 1930s, these two men fought each other for control of the nation. During the war they formed a sort of détente to help expel the invader. Once the Japanese were defeated a major civil war resumed. Mao was the eventual winner and took control of China by 1949. From the American view the worldwide balance of power was truly out of kilter, and we now faced problems as great as those encountered during World War II.

Republicans had generally supported our European commitment after 1945. The threat of Soviet expansion into Europe outweighed any reason for lessening our commitment. Our stance towards Asia was different. Right or wrong, our direction was towards Europe. Controversy over this position, which had been questioned by some members of the Republican party, exploded into anger when the Nationalists were defeated and forced to retreat to Formosa off the Chinese coast. Republicans focused their attacks on Truman's policy, since he had initially encouraged Chiang with military assistance in 1948 and 1949. GOP criticism became even more shrill when Truman refused to defend Formosa until the beginning of the Korean War. Essentially, bipartisanship did not operate effectively during the late 1940s vis-à-vis the Far East. The American people and leaders faced an even greater challenge in 1950, again in the Far East, with China as a principal player and Communist aggression spilling over its boundaries.

KOREA, TRUMAN, AND THE REPUBLICAN RESPONSE

The loss of China had made many Republicans wary of Truman and his policies in Asia. The general Republican feeling was that the administration had been too soft in dealing with Communist advances. China was only one part of a much larger picture for Republicans. Even though events overseas were important, some significant circumstances were also evolving on the domestic front within the GOP leadership.

No matter who led the minority opposition in the Senate, the center of power still rested with Truman at the White House and the Democratic majority on Capitol Hill. Their very will to use the forces of power was tested on June 25, 1950, when North Korea invaded South Korea. The Cold War rapidly escalated into a direct, armed confrontation between the Communist and free worlds. In many respects, Korea seemed an unlikely spot for a war. A small nation, apart from the Western world, quickly became the focal point of free world resistance to Communist expansion. The containment policy faced its severest test and the United Nations was used as the vehicle to impede the Communist threat.

Truman faced even tougher choices when it came to war policy. Essentially they broke down into three categories: (1) allow the area to go under Communist control, (2) fight a major war like World War II and use atomic weapons, and (3) fight a limited war, with limited objectives. His choice was the last, but it was not a policy for which the nation had been prepared.

Some authors, like Ronald Caridi in an article entitled "The GOP and the Korean War," argue that the early signs of the Korean involvement saw Republicans fairly united. Twenty-two senators out of forty-two spoke favorably about our Korean action during the first two weeks of the crisis.[15] Taft moved to the forefront of Republican antagonists for a variety of reasons; the most notable of which was Vandenberg's death in 1951. This void left Taft as the spokesman for Republican principles. Although Taft's expertise was seemingly never in foreign affairs (he usually deferred to Vandenberg in policy committee meetings), he became more vocal as Korean hostilities progressed.

According to his book on foreign policy, Taft was disturbed by the dualism in American policy during the early postwar period. He believed the same policy used for Europe should have been applied to Asia: "to check communism at every possible point where it is within our capacity to do so."[16] Taft had expressed some grave concerns over the direction of United States foreign policy in the 1930s and 1940s prior to our entering World War II. He saw war as an enemy of American liberty and our constitutional principles. The situation was further aggravated because war made the president nearly a dictator, weakened congressional power, distorted the economy, and diverted attention from domestic affairs. These premises, of course, reflect influence from his father who had advocated the Taftian-Contractual Theory in relation to presidential power. This theory held there was no residual power in the executive; rather, one must always look to the Constitution for guidance in relation to executive control. Naturally, the president's role would have to be limited in this area if one followed this analysis. The controversy, not unusual in American history, was how to interpret the gray area which comprised the undefined region of executive power in foreign affairs. FDR and Truman saw it from their perspective, and this became a focal point of confrontation with the intellectual, philosophical Taft. His two qualifications for this nation entering a war were quite simple: (1) "to protect the liberty of the people of the United States," and (2) "only second to liberty is the maintenance of peace."[17] His abounding fear was that the United States would overextend itself within a global context and develop some sort of *Pax Americana*. Even stronger, though, was the belief that we should go to war only in order to protect the national interest. That was the problem in the early 1950s; what was in the national interest?

However, the Republicans were quick to seize upon the idea that Harry Truman had taken unprecedented actions during this crisis, measures which constituted acts of war by the United States. Questions over legalities were raised by Republicans in the Senate as a result of the president's methods, but essentially the problem centered on the fact that they had not been consulted. The questions seemed to boil down to constitutional issues: advice and consent over international relations by the Senate and the war power which was to be exercised by the Congress.

Taft was caught in a quandary, since he supported the early stages of Korean involvement but believed that Secretary of State Dean Acheson should have resigned because—according to the Republican view—he had placed Korea outside the U.S. security line during a speech. The only logical conclusion for Taft was that this action had helped precipitate the Korean invasion. But Taft's partisan emotions were at work after the Korean War began and his inconsistency on foreign affairs became apparent when he was "caught amid his anticommunist militancy about Asia, his lifelong hostility toward extensive overseas involvement, and his partisan opposition to Truman."[18]

If these problems were not enough, Truman decided to fight a limited war with limited objectives. Although this was antithetical to the American military experience, it became policy because there was a fear Communist China would enter the conflict with overwhelming force, thereby prompting use of American atomic power. The eventual confrontation over this policy centered around General Douglas MacArthur, who commanded United Nations forces in Korea, and his commander in chief, Harry Truman. MacArthur advocated nothing short of complete victory and began to publicly state such feelings. Consequently, Truman relieved him of command, and the entire issue became a rallying point for Republicans. Taft entered the fray when he gave MacArthur full support after Truman relieved him of command and even served as an advisor to the general when he prepared to testify before Congress. Taft was also instrumental in arranging MacArthur's speech before a joint session of Congress.[19] When MacArthur returned to the United States after his dismissal, he was received by an anxious nation ready to shower him with praise as a hero. One author claims that this outpouring of adoration was more than hero worship. "This almost hysterical reception was primarily the result of the nation's frustration with the containment policy, which was psychologically and emotionally in contradiction with American values and experience in foreign affairs."[20]

The 1950 midterm elections were the first held since China had fallen to Mao, the rise of McCarthyism, the end of America's monopoly with atomic weapons, and the Korean War. It was also a time when bipartisanship began to disintegrate. There was a growing sense too—among Republicans and many other citizens—that containment was not working. Truman lost a number of supporters, especially senators, and the GOP made gains as foreign policy became the central issue for 1951 and beyond.[21]

All of these factors made the Senate into a countervailing source of power as Republican attacks continued upon Truman's administration. There had been a shift in the GOP from the internationalist wing, led by Vandenberg, to the more traditional and predominantly midwestern conservative interests championed by Taft. The latter group, in some cases, saw political expediency in attacking policies previously supported in the bipartisan tradition. The public, however, also accused Truman of foreign policy failure, and the opposition made the most of the rising anxiety within America's electorate. John Spanier has termed this situation as one which placed "American diplomacy in a domestic political straight jacket."[22] The concentration on domestic issues by Taft Republicans and their need to attack big government, economic constraints, increasing taxes, and a strong presidency led them to see foreign policy issues as a consequence of government misguided by internationalist Democrats. This excessively self-limiting view restrained the GOP from becoming a broadly positive force during the early postwar period. In a sense, it was a reaction to the world and domestic scene rather than a realization that fundamental changes had occurred and would continue.

As a people, we are accustomed to quick solutions in a military or political sense. Asia would not fit this mold or stereotype. The conservative wing of the Republican party went after Truman claiming "pro-Communist" sympathies which resulted in the loss of China. For Taft, Joseph McCarthy, and Richard Nixon, the problems were at home and not in the Far East. Scapegoats were necessary because we faced new frustrations. Our power, our omnipotence as a world force, was in question. For most Americans the problem had to be internal.

In effect, the people wanted a return to the use of destructive force so that the "enemy" might be crushed. In the atomic age, though, this was not possible. The postwar period between 1945 and 1952 and the ongoing Korean War severely tested our containment policy, the role of limited warfare, bipartisanship, and American political institutions. This period also served as a precursor for the Republican party as it sought to function as the loyal opposition nearly twenty-five years into the future. Korea too was a prelude of war to come in Asia, and that second experience would become the longest war in American history. The place: Vietnam.

EISENHOWER: REPUBLICAN ASCENDANCY AND DECLINE

Harry Truman declined another term as his party's nominee for president despite American participation in the Korean conflict.

Even though Truman sought some Republican input on foreign affairs, he was severely criticized by the GOP's platform in 1952. One of the main elements of this criticism centered on Asia; he was blamed for the loss of China, for moving "us into war with Korea without the consent of our citizens through their authorized representatives in the Congress, and for fighting without will to victory!"[23] Nevertheless, victory was to grace the GOP in another way. A small-town boy from Kansas was about to enter the White House and replace the son of a Missouri farmer. War hero, five-star general, supreme commander of Allied forces in Europe during World War II, were all adjectives used to describe Dwight D. Eisenhower, America's new president in 1953.

For many, Dwight Eisenhower represented the "grandfather image" in national politics. His election against Adlai Stevenson of Illinois was nearly assured; that fact brought joy to rank-and-file Republicans who felt rejuvenated after twenty years of Democratic rule from the White House. Thomas Bailey, noted American diplomatic historian, has written: "Eisenhower, with wide experience abroad, represented the internationalist wing of his party. Taft represented the isolationist or 'Dinosaur Wing,' which Democratic critics charged was attempting to 'repeal the 20th Century' ".[24] With the selection of Eisenhower as president, congressional Republicans who had internationalist leanings were virtually assured a sympathetic ear in reference to their foreign policy concerns. It is interesting to note that during a period of nearly four decades, Eisenhower would be the only Republican to hold the White House. On Capitol Hill the situation had a more profound twist; the GOP would only control Congress from 1949 to 1954 and again between 1953 and 1954, but this would be within a time frame of more than fifty years.

During the 1952 campaign, a cleavage appeared within Republican ranks. Bob Taft was apparently pushing for wider military action in Korea, but by June, Eisenhower broke with Taft's stance and refused to advocate an escalation of the war. In his view, seeking a military victory might risk a more general war outside Korea.[25] Truman had requested, in the period before the national conventions, that Korea be kept out of the presidential campaign. Republicans generally ignored this plan seizing upon the idea that war in Asia would become a predominant issue by the November elections. Eisenhower's attitudes about Korea remained fairly constant during this election period. His beliefs fell into three categories: first, that the administration had stumbled into Korea; second, once Communist forces had attacked, we were forced to intervene because isolationism was no longer viable as a policy; finally, total war in Korea had to be avoided.[26] MacArthur may have wanted a war on the Asian continent carried into mainland China, but Eisenhower rejected that solution as well as the desire to use atomic weapons.

Eisenhower, like most other chief executives in our history, was not without his set of crises, problems of state, or perplexing issues concerning foreign affairs. All of these factors were part of the price one pays for being president, and the former General of the Army was to face a situation resembling that of his predecessor. Just as Truman had witnessed events moving in Asia—and tried to shape or alter that trend—it was Eisenhower's turn as witness, and the location was Southeast Asia.

As we noted earlier, Asia generally had been destabilized as a result of World War II. China succumbed to Communist control in 1949, and war broke out in Korea during 1950, but the emphasis of American military power was directed towards preventing Soviet intervention in Western Europe. Disturbing events in Southeast Asia forced us to turn our attention towards that region.

Ironically, during the first half of the twentieth century our interests in Southeast Asia, or Indochina, were extremely limited. Demonstrative of our narrow political interests were the diplomatic arrangements with this area. There was a high commissioner and consulate in Manila, and nothing above them in eight other cities within Southeast Asia prior to World War II. Economically, our interests were concentrated in the Philippines. Some exports, such as tin and rubber, came from the East Indies and Malaysia; petroleum investment in Indonesia was also of some importance. We also sought to maintain air and supply routes through this region of the world.[27]

During World War II, Southeast Asia grew in importance because of its mineral wealth and close geographic proximity to Australia. The goal between 1941 and 1945 was to keep the Japanese away from Australia and to isolate this region of Asia from Japanese supplies. Most of the nations which made up Indochina had been under colonial domination of European powers, and, when World

War II ended, numerous local movements which had fought Japanese control sought to remove their European rulers. France, in particular, was caught up in a colonial war beginning in 1946 with its former colony of Vietnam. As colonial rule subsided, or was forcibly removed, the forces of self-determination and nationalism were already at work within Southeast Asia and Vietnam. It would be foolish to deny that agents from foreign governments and subversive techniques were being used in conjunction with nationalistic aspirations, but the basic indigenous feeling was to remove colonial rule.

Norman Graebner has theorized that we failed to recognize the forces of nationalism and change within Asia during the postwar period. Vietnam was divided among sects and most of them sought relief from French control. The more militant strain of Vietnamese citizens was led by Marxist organizer Ho Chi Minh. Even with the heavy French commitment of support for Vietnamese emperor Bao Dai, this outside military force could not prevent revolutionary change from taking place. Graebner has quoted the astute political observer, Walter Lippman, to illustrate the problem in Vietnam, or anywhere for that matter:

But to apply the methods of domestic politics to international politics is like using rules of checkers in a game of chess. Within a democratic state, conflicts are decided by an actual or a potential count of votes—as the saying goes, by ballots rather than bullets. But in a world of sovereign states conflicts are decided by power, actual or potential, for the ultimate is not an election but war.[28]

The United States paid scant attention to the situation in Vietnam between 1945 and 1950. Democracy seemed the only answer in Indochina, but our domestic situation and solutions were not necessarily appropriate to the rest of the world. Two events forced us to look at this region and take note of the problems; the first was the fall of Chiang Kai-shek in China and the second was Korea.

While the French attempted to reestablish their control in Southeast Asia—specifically Vietnam—the United States aided their effort financially, up to 75 percent of the war cost was borne by the United States, but we never intervened militarily. Vietnam's internal situation had diverse political, social, and economic factors which helped feed the Communist guerrilla movement led by Ho Chi Minh. These internal diversities were never resolved and France became embroiled in a major ground war. By the summer of 1953 the Korean War was over and Communist matériel from that front was heading south to aid Ho Chi Minh. The French, fighting insurgency since the end of World War II, were trying to win a ground war in their former colony with American aid. We had pledged support amounting to $358 million by December 1953.[29]

The French position with Indochina concerned Eisenhower. He did not want to see the area fall under Communist domination, but he did not want to intervene unless absolutely necessary. Instead of using the term containment, Republicans preferred to change the name—and in some cases the policy—to massive retaliation. Chief architect of the American response to communism in the 1950s was John Foster Dulles, Eisenhower's secretary of state. Both men wanted to align the free world against the evils of communism, and Eisenhower, early in his presidency, coined the term "domino theory," which he sought to apply to Asia. Essentially, it meant that if one nation fell to Marxism, others near it would fall like a house of cards or dominoes.

Besides the semantics of containment, Eisenhower also faced a new policy decision over national defense. The president was convinced that neither the economy nor the citizenry could stand wars of attrition such as Korea. Limited wars were not part of our military tradition and they were exasperating for the politicians. In the early part of his first term, he adopted a cost-efficient way of combining the national defense. Strategic weapons were developed with a capacity to deliver massive retaliation. There was also a redefinition of our defense perimeter. Democrats had drawn this security line from Norway to Turkey; Republicans under Eisenhower stretched the line to the Mideast and Far East.[30] The actual use of massive retaliation was left deliberately vague in order that Communist governments would be forced to think twice before expanding their perimeters. In this way, Eisenhower moved away from limited conventional wars while at the same time reinforcing an essential element of containment which was to keep communism within its borders.[31] With all of this in mind, Eisenhower turned his attention towards the problem of Vietnam.

President Eisenhower was not totally unfamiliar with the troubles in Vietnam. As early as 1951, he had pressed the French to declare that they did not wish to recolonize the area. The French refused, fearing it would weaken their control over the situation and lead to problems in other French possessions. The French government sought direct American military assistance, but Eisenhower demurred for various reasons; however, he did agree to send two hundred Air Force technicians from mid-February to mid-June of 1954. He did not take the step, though, without consulting Congress.

The test for Eisenhower's philosophy of indirect intervention came in 1954. Author Robert Divine has written that Eisenhower had four basic assumptions concerning Indochina and American security interests. First, the region was a geographic and mineral resource for that part of Asia. Second, he believed that the French had positioned themselves improperly after World War II by not allowing for Vietnamese liberation and self-government. In a similar vein, they did not include other Asians in this struggle against communism. Third, allied support from other nations was needed; otherwise it would appear that we were acting as a colonial power. The final assumption rested on Eisenhower's concept of executive leadership. Congress, under the Constitution, held the war power, and he did not want to be called a hypocrite, since Republicans had viciously attacked Truman for his unilateral moves in Korea. Congress, not the president, was to grant extra steps in our military commitment.[32] This last part deserves a bit more comment. Divine argues that Eisenhower understood the political reality within the United States. There was strong congressional opposition, ironically from two Democrats. Senators John F. Kennedy and Lyndon B. Johnson expressed shock and concern that the administration was considering another land war in Asia.

In a recently published book entitled *Eisenhower*, Stephen Ambrose goes into further depth on the political reality. He writes:

A major theme of Eisenhower's campaign had been a rejection of containment and an adoption of a policy of liberation. Now the Republicans had been in power for more than a year. They had failed to liberate any Communist slave anywhere. Indeed in Korea they had accepted an armistice that left North Korea in Communist hands. Eisenhower was keenly aware that by far his most popular act had been to achieve peace in Korea, but he was just as aware that Republican orators had been demanding to

know ever since 1949, "Who lost China?" Could he afford to allow Democrats to ask "Who lost Vietnam?" He told his Cabinet he could not.[33]

The most recent scholarship from Ambrose indicates that President
Eisenhower constructed a support system within the United States
in order to cover his political position, because there would be
tremendous demands for American intervention once the French
lost. His strategy was simple: place conditions on American involvement which, by design, were impossible to fulfill. Ambrose
outlines them as follows: (1) a French grant of independence to
Vietnam, (2) British participation in any military action, (3) some
of the other nations in Southeast Asia were to be involved, (4) prior
and complete approval from Congress, (5) the French would turn
war strategy over to the United States, but their troops would
remain in the field for combat, and (6) the French had to prove we
were not there to cover their withdrawal.[34] These conditions, of
course, were never met, so direct military intervention from our
side never took place. Eisenhower, as we saw earlier, did not want
America to be viewed as a colonial power, but he did wish to form
a regional group for the purposes of collective security. Dulles
broadened the idea through the development of the Southeast Asia
Treaty Organization, what was later called SEATO.

Despite the technical and financial assistance from the United
States, French forces capitulated to Communist troops. The final
battle was characterized by heavy losses on both sides. The French
surrendered their position on May 7, 1954, at Dien Bien Phu.
Formal discussions over Vietnam's future were hammered out in
an agreement known as the Geneva accords. Separate truce agreements were signed during July 1954 for South Vietnam and the
neighboring nations of Cambodia and Laos. Vietnam was divided—
similar to Korea—at the seventeenth parallel. The Vietminh (Communist forces) were given control of the northern part, while the
southern territory became the Republic of Vietnam. For a period
of three hundred days during the truce, people would be allowed
to move between the northern and southern portions of the country.
Supervision of this agreement rested with a group entitled the International Control Commission, which included representatives
from India, Poland, and Canada. Elections were to be held during
July 1956 under the commission's direction. There were no sig-

natories to these accords; rather, the participants took a voice vote and agreed to follow the guidelines. The United States and South Vietnam consented not to upset the accords by military force.[35]

Once the geographic division of Vietnam was under way a new leader was chosen to direct governmental affairs in Saigon, the new capital of the southern region. His name was Ngo Dinh Diem, and he was selected by the absent Bao Dai in June 1954. Diem came from a highly prominent Catholic family and had total trust in no one except his closest relatives. His style of leadership was autocratic and paranoic, extremely poor qualities for a South Vietnamese leader.

Eisenhower gave Diem support and credence when he sent the premier a letter in October 1954 pledging American assistance with the implicit understanding that numerous domestic reforms would have to take place under his regime. However, Diem was a reluctant follower, and he refused to hold national elections, as stipulated by the Geneva accords, under the argument that Vietnam should be totally unified. America acquiesced to this position under the theory "that it was more important for the Saigon regime to be strong and anticommunist than democratic."[36] We even carried this a step further and doubled the American military contingent in Saigon to 685 men during the spring of 1956.

Our primary fear during the early years of the Eisenhower administration was quite simple: Communist expansion within Southeast Asia was unacceptable, just as it had been in Korea. China was still viewed as the subversive agent spreading Marxist doctrine throughout Asia. Consequently, we increased our commitment to Vietnam in order to contain communism, but the commitment was decidedly more limited than our Korean experience. In order to enhance the stability of this region, we adopted collective security through the use of SEATO. The fundamental fact, however, was that Indochina demonstrated that outside military force *could not* prevent revolutionary change from within. The situation has been described by Norman Graebner:

The Indochina civil war, raging since 1946, went steadily against the French. Observers on the scene understood clearly that the strength of the revolutionary forces of Ho Chi Minh sprang from the nationalistic fervor of the countryside, implemented by rebel promises and fear of reprisal as well as the general desire of the masses to rid the country of French rule. But

to Washington officials the fact that Ho was an avowed Communist reduced the civil war, aimed primarily at national independence and so regarded by the countries of Asia, to a communist aggression emanating
from Peking.[37]

Graebner has argued that official Washington could not see the
writing on the wall. But Eisenhower in his memoirs stated that if
other nations in Southeast Asia were unwilling to commit their
forces to that locality then we should reappraise our security policy.
He did believe intervention would have been necessary if China
had directly entered the fighting, but even then we should not have
carried the entire security burden. Years later, Eisenhower stated
his basic feelings: "Willingness to fight for freedom, no matter
where the battle may be, has always been a characteristic of our
people, but the conditions then prevailing in Indochina were such
as to make unilateral American intervention nothing less than sheer
folly."[38]

DOMESTIC POLITICS AND EISENHOWER

By January 1953, Eisenhower was in the White House and later
that year accepted a settlement which partitioned Korea at the thirty-
eighth parallel and created a generally unsettled condition in Asia.
This plan was similar to one proposed by Truman, but even some
Republicans found this idea unacceptable. Conservative senators
such as Taft, William Jenner of Indiana, and Joseph McCarthy of
Wisconsin resented the idea of a stalemate based on the military
position from 1950. These senators were more interested in winning
the war and carrying the fight to China. Since these views were
espoused by the conservative wing of the Republican party—a group
with limited political clout—Eisenhower was able to resist their
demands. As he sought to end the American fighting commitment
in Korea, other events were unfolding which had implications for
America's domestic and foreign policy.

During the 1950s congressional politics had taken a turn for the
better as far as Republicans were concerned. As noted earlier, for
the second time in twenty years the GOP controlled both houses
of Congress, and with a Republican in the White House the future
seemed bright since policy would develop through a new majority.

But Eisenhower was not Taft's choice for the presidency, and the early years of Eisenhower's first term saw continued haggling between the White House and Capitol Hill Republicans. One instance was an exception to this trend and ironically it came from the Senate.

When Eisenhower took office, some Republican members of the Senate wished to minimize friction with the new administration. Prior to 1953 the Republican Policy Committee gained prominence as a voice for party concerns. Since one of its own was occupying the White House, cooperation was to be the order of the day. A regular report to the policy committee was given by the Republican Senate leaders normally on the day of a weekly meeting with the president. Since total agreement with Eisenhower was impossible, these meetings served to increase the understanding between the White House and Republicans, provided more concise information to the senators, and helped to form mutual agreements in some cases.[39] In order to give extra credence to these policy committee meetings, Vice President Nixon or one of the cabinet members would be present. These changes from 1953 on were indicative of how policy was to be made. The focus was on the president, and Republican congressional leaders found it necessary to assume a lower profile. If serious divisions arose among Republican senators, the policy committee and the White House sought some form of compromise. By 1956 all Republican senators were allowed to attend these meetings. Demands by liberal elements within GOP ranks forced a change which gave all Republicans direct access to the leadership reports of their meetings with the president.

Even with these changes in Senate political organization there was still some friction between Eisenhower and other party members. Unanimity in politics is nearly impossible, but the inherent nature of Republican sympathies towards internationalist or isolationist tendencies splintered the overall party structure. Eisenhower had to contend with this phenomenon, and by 1956 Democrats regained lost ground winning a majority in Congress. This reversal shifted greater emphasis on White House proposals and initiatives since they were the only Republican branch of government to be found in Washington. Whether or not Republicans held a majority in Congress, it became increasingly difficult to maintain party unity. Holbert Carroll, in his book *The House of*

Representatives and Foreign Policy, notes that the situation changed in the House:

The number of Republican conference sessions declined sharply. Despite this more positive leadership, the Republican leaders, whether as majority leaders in the Eighty-third Congress (1953–1954) or as minority leaders in the Eighty-fourth Congress (1955–1956), were not able to coordinate party attitudes in foreign affairs as effectively as the Democrats. The Democrats suffered an erosion of their unity and strength in these four years, but deeper division persisted in Republican ranks and the President was not disposed to exert strong political leadership over his congressional party.[40]

It was difficult, therefore, to compel unity in the GOP ranks. The role of key Republican leaders in the House and Senate was more persuasive in nature. Sanctions against members were nearly meaningless. Even key GOP leaders in committees exerted some influence, and at least one author has argued that this group functioned as a compromising and communications agent with the White House.[41]

When Republicans were in power or out, divisions still plagued their membership in Congress. Republicans from the coastal regions of the nation gave Eisenhower nearly unanimous support for overseas aid programs while those from the western and plains states voted against most foreign aid measures in nearly the same way they had against Truman's requests. This cleavage could be extended or explained further on a regional basis. Internationalism was consistently strong from those Republicans who represented the West Coast or northeastern areas of the United States.[42] What helped Eisenhower, though, was a growing amount of bipartisan support from the Democrats. Even with the GOP split, Eisenhower was still able to consolidate a Republican commitment to major foreign policies which had been developed through Democratic initiatives. This support was usually seen in areas such as the United Nations and the Marshall Plan.

Part of the cohesiveness, then, in the 1950s was Eisenhower himself. The power and prestige of the presidency went a long way in healing some inherent philosophical divisions that had plagued the party since the early postwar period and even before World War II. But there was another significant force, and it was to be found in the Congress. Two men entered key leadership positions for the Republican party on Capitol Hill during the 1950s. Their names were Charles A. Halleck of Indiana and Everett McKinley Dirksen of Illinois. Once again, two midwestern conservatives were chosen to help direct their party's affairs within Congress.

Tough, pragmatic, shrewd, and intelligent were adjectives appropriately applied to Charlie Halleck and Ev Dirksen. Each man had a perspective of American destiny which had been nurtured by similar experiences; both men played the American game of politics with finesse. Halleck, a congressman from northwestern Indiana, was the epitome of the state's conservative strain. A lawyer by profession, Halleck graduated first in his law class at Indiana University. He worked in his parents' legal firm and served as a prosecuting attorney for ten years before winning a special election in 1935 to fill a vacant congressional post. Halleck represented the old second district of Indiana which stretched from the southern shores of Lake Michigan to the city of Lafayette and Tippecanoe County. A superb orator, Halleck delivered "barn-burning" speeches within his home state (which were as good if not better than Hoosier basketball games) and seemingly felt at ease either in the power circles of Washington or the second district.

Halleck became majority leader in the House from 1947 to 1949 and from 1953 to 1955 and in the interim years the minority leader. After the GOP loss in the 1956 election, he would not hold a leadership position again until 1959. Thereafter, he remained as minority leader until defeated in a conference vote in 1965. Some people considered him more conservative than Eisenhower, but years later Halleck would state that Eisenhower was the greatest president under whom he had ever served.[43]

Everett Dirksen was Halleck's counterpart in the Senate. Dirksen, raised on a central Illinois farm, was a veteran of World War I when he returned to his hometown of Pekin and began a political career several years later. He was elected to the U.S. House in 1932 and stayed until 1948. An eye ailment forced him to leave Congress; however, he returned to Washington two years later after winning a senatorial seat from Illinois in 1950. During the 1940s, Dirksen aligned himself with the isolationist wing of the Republican party. In 1952 he supported Bob Taft for the presidential nomination and openly attacked Thomas E. Dewey at the national convention.

Dewey, who had been the GOP nominee for president in 1944 and 1948, was chastised by Dirksen for leading the GOP to defeat. However, Dewey's choice for president—and not surprisingly, the choice of many others—was Eisenhower. Dirksen was not to achieve a leadership position in the Congress until January 1957 when he became the Senate's minority whip. He began supporting Eisenhower, more than before, in a political sense by this time and eventually became the minority leader in 1959. He held this post until his death in 1969.

Halleck was not the only midwestern politician who gave excellent speeches. Dirksen, too, was an imposing individual. His mane of gray hair, deep Shakespearean voice, and use of the dramatic pause aroused his listeners on many occasions. Dirksen was the master politician when the time came for patriotic movement, and he was known throughout the nation for his renditions, or quotations, from fundamental American documents. In short, his eloquence, ability to move people, and political skill were superb.

Republican political fortunes ebbed and flowed during the 1950s. Their political control of Congress came only in limited stints. After 1957 the GOP was relegated to a secondary position politically within the Congress. By holding the White House, the mainstream of the GOP felt more assured that their ideas, beliefs, and values would be articulated into policy. Without a doubt, Eisenhower faced criticism from the right wing of his party, but he sensed a need for unification and called for a reexamination of Republican programs and philosophy after the midterm elections of 1958. In 1959 a committee on programs and progress was established to examine party philosophy. Richard Nixon, Eisenhower's two-term vice president, was given charge over the evaluative efforts. Charles Percy, later to be elected as a senator from Illinois, was picked to chair these groups. Of course, Eisenhower was attempting to set the stage for a Republican election victory in 1960, but he also must have felt that if the GOP was defeated in its bid to retain the White House, party mechanisms would have to take over in order to exert influence over domestic and foreign policy.

THE PRESIDENTIAL ELECTION OF 1960

Constitutionally, Eisenhower was denied from seeking a third term. This, coupled with his health—he had suffered a heart at-

tack—made it impossible for him to continue as president. Therefore, 1960 was to be the setting for a race for the White House by
numerous politicians, but the field was finally narrowed to two
men: Richard M. Nixon and John F. Kennedy. This presidential
election was to be the watershed for America's internal direction
and the direction of foreign affairs, especially in places like Vietnam.

One of the major issues during the campaign was America's
international role. Kennedy attacked the Republican administration
for failing to respond to events in Cuba, Africa, and Asia. Fidel
Castro, a Communist, took control of Cuba in the late 1950s. Many
regions were experiencing left-wing political movements, and the
rise of Castro was more than mere political embarrassment for
Dwight Eisenhower. Castro represented the first Communist government in the Western Hemisphere, and to add insult to injury he
was ninety miles off the Florida coast. Kennedy's indictment against
Eisenhower's policy towards these international problems came in
a speech during September 1960 in which he said, "[E]arly and
effective action by the United States could have headed off the crisis
that had developed."[44] Kennedy was also eager to point out that
Vice President Nixon had been in each country before problems
boiled over.

Above and beyond the political rhetoric, Democrats were not
really divided on foreign policy and defense issues in this campaign.
However, they had to deal with racial, religious, and leadership
issues. Civil rights struggles would peak in the 1960s. Kennedy's
Catholicism and youthful appearance were handicaps which the
party and its presidential nominee were forced to overcome. Kennedy addressed the issue of religion in a straightforward manner;
his physical appearance was another matter. For some, Kennedy
looked young, acted young, and therefore did not have the background to lead. While Democrats had their tussles, Republicans
were not far behind with their set of antagonizing problems.

According to author Theodore White, in his award-winning book
Making of the President 1960, Nelson Rockefeller was the most significant "disruptive" influence for Republicans during the 1960 race.
The New York governor, a member of one of the nation's wealth-
iest families, also harbored presidential ambitions. Rockefeller's main
concern seemed to be national defense. He claimed that B–47s and
B–52s operated under the threat of potential destruction

by the Soviet Union. This was epitomized by a so-called missile gap which Kennedy also used as a charge against Republicans. Rockefeller also advocated major defense expenditures of $3 billion to help remedy our strategic posture.[45]

There was a feeling, in some quarters, that Rockefeller's charges and pleadings were a direct repudiation of Eisenhower's policies. But the New York governor, a GOP moderate, had been advocating changes within the party anyway. For some, his position was just more progressive than anything else. Curiously enough, Nixon essentially agreed with most of Rockefeller's points. The governor, though, refused to yield on his ideas during the summer convention. Charles Percy, chairman of the platform committee, tried to bridge the various factions but could not break the deadlock. The mood between the two Republican groups has been characterized by White as follows: "But the philosophy behind all of them was one of urgency. All rested on the assumption that a great government must not only deal with situations as-they-are but go on to change, by its own initiative, the frame of problems or the machinery to deal with them."[46]

Obviously, Republicans needed to compromise on an essential issue: national defense. In deference to this spirit of mutual cause, Nixon secretly flew to New York City during the early hours of Friday, July 22, 1960. While dining with Rockefeller, the vice president tried to sway his host by offering him the second spot on the GOP ticket. The governor refused, but an agreement between the two men was reached, known as the Compact of Fifth Avenue, which contained fourteen points—seven of which dealt with foreign policy and national defense.

The Republican platform of 1960 made numerous references to a fight with communism and the need for economic and educational development of nations within Asia and Latin America. Republicans also declared themselves open to other nations that sought self-determination.

In Latin America, Asia, Africa, and the Middle East, peoples of ancient and recent independence have shown their determination to improve their standards of living, and to enjoy an equality with the rest of mankind in the enjoyment of the fruits of civilization. This determination has become a primary fact of their political life. We declare ourselves to be in sympathy with their aspiration.[47]

Many of the Republican rank and file considered the compact as a sellout to Rockefeller; yet Nixon could not afford to offend Eisenhower or the party regulars and hope to keep the GOP intact. Nixon based his acceptance of Rockefeller's ideas on the need for political harmony. Although he had the stamp of legitimacy after serving under Eisenhower for eight years, Nixon had to contend with the various wings of the party in 1960 which were still split philosophically.

The decade after Eisenhower was to be a decisive one for the United States. America's new leadership would face a series of challenges both domestic and foreign. These fundamental issues were reflected in our politics. A profound concern over Soviet intentions still permeated American society. Sputnik, the first satellite into space and coincidentally belonging to the Russians, influenced the emphasis on math and science in school curriculums so much that a second-place syndrome infected the nation. In all of this, politics would respond; it had to since the very nature of the American political system forced this kind of confrontation.

Republicans, too, faced a series of choices during the 1960s. All their attempts at compromise failed to give Nixon the White House or even majority control in Congress. The defeat, no matter how narrow or wide, forced Republicans into a role all too familiar since World War II: that of a loyal opposition. So, just as the United States would face domestic and foreign challenges, the GOP would be tied intrinsically to these events. Everett Dirksen wrote in late 1959 that America had been through "its seventh year since the end of the Korean War in which no American boys were engaged in foreign wars."[48] Unfortunately, Dirksen's vision could not foresee beyond 1959. Conflict in South Vietnam was to be *the significant* foreign policy issue of the forthcoming decade. All Americans would be affected, and the Republican party was about to face a serious challenge for the minority political party within our system: how to respond to an overseas war of limited engagement coupled with serious domestic turmoil on the home front. This was the party's essential challenge, which it sought to meet beginning in 1961.

2.

THE EV AND CHARLIE SHOW VS. JFK

In January 1961, the overall world situation was indeed menacing for America's newly elected chief of state. John F. Kennedy entered office as the cauldron of world affairs began to boil over. Africa, Berlin, Cuba, and Southeast Asia were all areas of concern for America's leaders. Relations with the Soviet Union were also tenuous and Kennedy addressed these international problems in his inaugural address. JFK had campaigned on a platform calling for new, decisive leadership; a realization of these burdens, with the leadership it entailed, shifted his way when he was sworn into office. However, he inherited his share of international crises from Dwight D. Eisenhower. Kennedy had to accept many conditions as they existed, carry out Eisenhower's policies, or develop new strategies for ongoing problems. It was in this context that he sought to chart American policies during his tenure at the White House. In a series of election speeches edited by historian Allan Nevins, the future president outlined his concerns to the nation. These speeches were categorized into various areas designed to give the citizenry a view of the Kennedy vision. Categories of economic, political, and social concerns were combined with statements about areas such as Vietnam and Southeast Asia. The irony here is that some of the ideas or beliefs that Kennedy espoused and to which he called attention were still being discussed twenty-five years later.

There are several useful guides that highlight Kennedy's method of decision making in the foreign policy arena. Roger Hilsman's work *To Move a Nation* and Theodore Sorensen's *Kennedy* detail the struggles JFK faced and how he sought solutions to numerous situations. According to Hilsman, Eisenhower had organized his administration so that his top advisors could give final approval to matters once they had been hashed out on a lower policy-making level. This kind of organizational structure promoted a "team concept"; the pressure for resolution was placed on the lower-level planner to reconcile policy differences.[1] Of course, Eisenhower held the final say over the direction of his foreign affairs goals especially with the plans for stemming Communist movements within the world.

Kennedy was an activist in foreign policy and his structure for decision making encompassed the State Department, close advisors, and his personal intervention. During a private meeting in early January 1961, Kennedy encouraged Hilsman to join his administration. The president-elect outlined his desire to develop strategies which counteracted the worldwide threat of Communist guerrilla warfare. Hilsman states Kennedy's conviction on this matter was simple: "[T]he most likely and immediate threat from the communists was neither nuclear war nor large-scale conventional wars, as in Korea, but the more subtle, ambiguous threat of the guerrilla."[2] Therefore, new military and political tactics had to be developed and deployed if the Marxist challenge was to be met. These new strategies would reflect the American activism with foreign affairs. A distinct appreciation for the "emerging peoples" and the subsequent nationalism arising in many nonaligned or poor nations were also part of JFK's new vision. The policy was to be determined by the president with some input from Congress. Republican rhetoric also played a role because Kennedy was acutely aware of Republican criticism. Ted Sorensen, who was one of the president's closest advisors, has written about the administration's intense concentration with international matters:

Foreign affairs had always interested him far more than domestic. They occupied far more of his time and energy as President. They received from him far more attention to detail, to the shaping of alternatives, to the course of a proposal from origin to execution. They tested far more severely his talents of judgment and execution, with far less emphasis on budget and legislative planning and far more occasions for reacting to unforeseeable and uncontrollable events.[3]

Numerous independent states were created as a result of World War II; many of them refused to align themselves with America or the Soviet Union during the Cold War. They viewed the two superpowers as rival contenders for dominance over their newly created nations. The United States incorrectly assumed that the rising nationalism would be a countervailing force against Marxism. The unpleasant reality, however, was just the opposite, and this fact became one of the most disturbing aspects of international relations for America during the postwar period. Consequently, Kennedy faced nationalistic movements arising in Africa and Asia while persistent problems continued with Berlin, Cuba, and the Soviet Union.

REPUBLICAN POLICY FORMATION

As has been noted, Kennedy faced numerous challenges in foreign affairs when he took office, but he also had to come to grips with a political challenge: Republicans as the loyal opposition. The personification of this opposition was found in the congressional leaders—Halleck and Dirksen. Each of these men had served with Kennedy during his congressional career. A curiosity in this relationship with Republicans in general, and with Halleck and Dirksen in particular, was noted by Sorenson:

But on foreign policy, civil rights and a few other issues, his good relations with conservative GOP leaders Dirksen and Halleck were rewarding. He liked both men, respected them as fellow professionals and enjoyed bantering with them over their successes and defeats. In fact, by 1962 his relations were so good with Dirksen—whom he had always found entertaining and at times movable by invocations of patriotism (or patronage)— that both men had to reassure their respective party members that each had not embraced the other too much.[4]

The two Republican leaders were formidable opponents, never to be taken for granted or trifled with. They commanded respect and Kennedy would have been foolish to discount their abilities to question, probe, and diminish policy decisions made by his administration.

The Republican strategy for opposing the new president took

shape prior to JFK receiving the reins of power. Shortly before
President Eisenhower left office, he summoned the congressional
leadership to the White House. During their meeting the president
noted that the GOP was about to lose control of the executive
branch. Historically, the responsibility for voicing Republican concerns usually went to the party leaders on Capitol Hill when the
Democrats controlled the presidency. In order to structure a firm
minority position for the future—and to allow for Eisenhower's
input—a joint Senate-House leadership group was created. The
objectives for this body were summed up as follows:

> The Republican leaders of the Senate and the House would form a joint
> group, to be known as the Joint Senate-House Republican Leadership,
> with the chairman of the Republican National Committee to act as pre-
> siding officer, to hold meetings approximately once a week, after which
> the Senate and House Republican leaders, as spokesmen, would hold a
> joint press conference for the newspaper, periodical, TV, and radio
> correspondents.
> When desirable, other appropriate GOP leaders would be invited to meet
> with the Joint Senate-House Republican Leadership.
> For the purpose of coordinating the effort, stimulating research, and
> carrying out of other administrative duties, President Eisenhower sug-
> gested the joint leadership be provided with a staff.[5]

Informal leadership meetings began on January 24, 1961, while a
record of formal statements was kept beginning on March 23. During this period, six other meetings were held. Between March and
September, additional discussions were convened with party leaders
such as Arizona Senator Barry Goldwater, Richard Nixon, and
New York Governor Nelson Rockefeller. The reason for including
these individuals was an awareness of the need to cement various
Republican wings into some kind of cohesive voice for national
policy.

Eisenhower's attempts to unify the party's voice and influence
from the congressional stance illustrated a new innovation within
Republican politics. It was a novel idea, but it also took a turn
towards the theatrical side. During a meeting of the Washington
Press Club, Halleck and Dirksen did a rendition for those present
and added some humor to the occasion. Columnist Tom Wicker
of the *New York Times* chose to call this the "Ev and Charlie Show."

Even though the joint leadership had met twenty-two times and held press conferences on each occasion, they were ridiculed in numerous segments of the press. The *Christian Science Monitor* dubbed the show "a 'cross between the Huntley-Brinkley NBC news broadcast and an old-fashioned minstrel show."[6]

According to one author, the theatrics also were taking a toll within the GOP ranks, and senators like George Aiken (Vermont), Barry Goldwater (Arizona), and Thruston Morton (Kentucky) openly criticized the show. Some feared a "prairie conservatism" was being displayed, thereby harming the overall Republican image.[7] This internal party feeling would be vented when the chairman of the conference was removed in early 1963 and eventually Halleck would be replaced as minority leader in 1965. With both of these changes Congressman Gerald Ford (Michigan) became a pivotal leader; first he assumed chairmanship of the conference and then moved to the minority leader's spot. Theatrics aside, these press conferences were designed to present alternatives to the Democratic policies and programs. In this vein, they were successful.

Although their main focus was domestic affairs, Halleck and Dirksen also spoke out about international relations. On March 22, 1961, the leadership issued a statement which served as a synopsis of the Eisenhower years. The essential elements of this overview were: (1) our defense posture was crucial to global peace; (2) this force, developed between 1953 and 1961, was responsible for preventing the outbreak of a war of major proportions; and (3) containing communism in local disputes was essential in our foreign affairs.[8] The Republican leadership also was quick to challenge the Soviets and did not hesitate to give JFK its views about his forthcoming meeting with Khrushchev in Vienna on June 3 and 4, 1961.

The prime reason why negotiations between the Soviet Union and the United States have almost always ended in failure is that the Soviets are negotiating for world domination while we have been negotiating for world peace. These are two completely incompatible objectives.[9]

The preceding quotation illustrates the tough public stance that Republican leaders took towards Soviet-American relations. On the surface it offered little compromise, if any. But there was a recurring theme during 1961 and it was simply stated by Halleck

and Dirksen: Kennedy had to be tough with the Soviets. According
to Dirksen, on June 8, "the only thing the Communists understand
is strength."[10]

During the first year of JFK's administration, the criticisms were
usually leveled against officials other than the president. Men such
as Ambassadors Averell Harriman and Chester Bowles, or even
members of the Democratic majority such as Senate Foreign Relations Chairman J. William Fulbright (D-Arkansas) faced the brunt
of Republican venom. Not surprisingly, this public stance for the
GOP was shunted away in the private world of politics. Kenneth
Crawford, in a *Newsweek* column entitled "The Loyal Opposition,"
noted that Republicans were giving basic support to Kennedy's
initiatives in foreign affairs because of policy positions formulated
during meetings of the Joint Republican Congressional Policy
Committee. It was Crawford's assertion that Eisenhower was in-
fluencing statements behind the scenes. He argued even further that:

> The two old troupers [Halleck and Dirksen] have contrived to be critical
> of the administration in what they have said while upholding its major
> foreign policies and the legislation necessary to carry them out in what
> they have left unsaid. The result has satisfied both the emotional Repub-
> licans, who are entertained by partisan gibes at the opposition, and the
> more sophisticated party men, who like to make a record for the next
> campaign but understand what the President and the country are up against
> in Berlin and elsewhere.[11]

During the early stage of the Kennedy presidency, Sorenson has
noted the strong evidence of bipartisanship. Some claimed that
Kennedy had no choice in accepting bipartisanship due to his narrow election victory, and Sorenson has written:

> But even had he been elected overwhelmingly, his foreign policy *objectives*,
> as distinguished from his *methods*, would not, I believe, have differed rad-
> ically from those of his Republican predecessor. He still would have as-
> signed many of the most controversial slots in national security to
> Republicans to diminish partisan division. His narrow margin of effective
> Congressional support, a by-product of that close election, did hamper his
> efforts on foreign aid and lesser problems.[12]

This spirit of bipartisanship was to be crucial for Kennedy, Republicans, and the nation as international developments began to unfold during 1961 and beyond.

Prior to assuming the presidency, Kennedy had campaigned on the notion of a "hard line" against Soviet expansionism. He also had chided Eisenhower for the supposed missile gap. JFK's reasoning for all of this was clear: he did not want to be classified as the appeaser. Therefore, his position as a "cold warrior" was established, and Republicans were going to make sure he stayed on course. His initial tests for this course came in three areas: Berlin, Cuba, and Southeast Asia.

For nearly two decades Berlin had been a focal point of disagreement and tension between the superpowers. Surrounded by East German territory, Berlin remained a divided city; Communist rule was imposed on the eastern side while capitalism flourished in the western zone. Soviet intentions had always been unclear, but it seemed reasonable to assume they would not allow Germany to unite under its former capital. For the Soviets, the specter of German unification meant an immediate threat to their western security zone. The Soviets, and their premier Nikita Khrushchev, were pushing for a separate peace treaty with Germany thereby removing the legitimacy of the government in Bonn, the new capital in West Germany. Herbert Parmet in his book *JFK*, which is a history of Kennedy's administration, has noted the president's desire to keep Berlin free. Parmet has further observed that Kennedy must have "had the nightmare of allowing Germany to become to Khrushchev what Poland became to Stalin in his dealings with FDR."[13]

Throughout 1961, Halleck and Dirksen publicly encouraged Kennedy to remain strong with U.S. resolve concerning Berlin. They hastened to add this commitment had to be maintained, not sidetracked with issues such as the admittance of Red China to the United Nations or domestic expenditures which GOP leaders felt must be trimmed if the defense budget was to increase; otherwise, challenges like Berlin could not be met. The Soviets did make several moves with Berlin; the most notable was closing off free access by East Berliners to the western zone. This action was accomplished by the infamous Berlin Wall which became symbolic of the struggle between freedom and servitude. Dirksen, speaking for the joint leadership, informed the nation about the Republican concern and support for American policy over this issue.

[L]et it be clearly understood that President Kennedy has the complete support of the Republican leadership in Congress in the Berlin crisis. If differences should appear, they would be on how to uphold our Berlin commitments, not whether to uphold them. We are all aware that the issue is not a city named Berlin, but free world unity.[14]

One month later, he chided the Democrats for speaking with a multitude of voices on Berlin. The senator from Illinois claimed these types of misstatements produced two results: "[T]hey weaken the bargaining position of the United States, and they dismay our friends and our allies by a display of contradictions and confusion."[15] Even though Berlin was important for the European-American alliance (NATO), an issue in the Western Hemisphere captured the headlines far more often than Germany's old capital.

Cuba, ninety miles off the Florida coast, had become a public embarrassment for the United States by 1961. Fidel Castro had established a Communist dictatorship in Cuba during the late 1950s. Eisenhower broke off diplomatic relations with Castro almost three weeks before Kennedy entered office. JFK had been briefed throughout the campaign about the persistent problems with Cuba and was also aware of the American plan to support an invasion of the island by Cuban nationals. Eisenhower, with advice and encouragement from Nixon, had approved a covert CIA operation to invade Cuba, remove Castro, and establish a democratic government.[16] Kennedy, much to his regret, allowed this plan to continue and on April 17, 1961, the Bay of Pigs invasion commenced. Several days later, the invading force was defeated, its remnants captured, and Kennedy accepted full responsibility for the failure.

In order to mute Republican criticism, Kennedy made several moves that helped insure a bipartisan front. First, he met with Eisenhower at Camp David and solicited his understanding and support, which came somewhat reluctantly. Privately, the former president was disturbed with the way Kennedy had handled himself, but he was crucial in helping temper Halleck's and Dirksen's remarks. The two congressional leaders wanted Eisenhower to hit hard at this failure; instead, he cautioned them against charges that would sound like McCarthyism.[17] Even Eisenhower was cautious in his response. When questioned by reporters after the Camp David meeting, he responded with the answer that he was "supporting the man who had to carry the responsibility for foreign affairs."[18] Publicly, at least, he sidestepped the issue about his actual feelings.

Kennedy's second step was to meet with Richard Nixon on April 20; from this discussion emerged another consensus, and the former vice president also urged bipartisan support for JFK. He publicly stated that those individuals with only scant information and details were irresponsible when criticizing the administration, especially if they were from outside the government.[19] Speaking before a dinner given in honor of the prime minister from Greece, Nixon related part of his conversation with Kennedy:

I told him that as a private citizen I would support him, and I believed the country would support him, if any proposals he would make, consistent with our international obligations, designed to stop further Communist penetration in this hemisphere, or in Asia, especially a further build-up of the Communist beachhead in Cuba and including, if he considered it necessary, the commitment of American armed forces.[20]

The third action initiated by the president was to meet with New York's illustrious governor, Nelson Rockefeller. After a one-hour meeting, Rockefeller announced that all Americans should "stand united behind the President in whatever action is necessary to defend freedom."[21]

Despite the outward unity of top Republican leaders, rumblings were emanating from Capitol Hill with a distinctly different tone. Senator Barry Goldwater (Arizona)—a presidential contender for 1964—claimed all Americans should have had "apprehension and shame" because the invasion failed. He further blamed the defeat upon the "ineptitude" of the State Department.[22] Another Republican senator, Kentucky's Thruston Morton, declared in a Senate speech that there was a lack of candor from the White House because it had refused early on to admit its complicity in the whole affair. The *New York Times* claimed that Morton's speech "shattered the political calm" in Washington.[23] New York's Republican senator, Jacob Javits, urged the use of economic aid as a tool for removing Castro by declaring we would send that aid once the Cuban people removed Castro. He also suggested that we invoke the terms of the Inter-American Treaty of 1947 to break diplomatic relations and establish economic sanctions by the signatories against Castro. His argument went further by advocating a unity that would eventually lead to the deployment of armed force if it became necessary.[24]

Nixon, stating once again the top leadership's position within the GOP, argued that his fellow Republicans should not publicly criticize the president for "mistakes which have hurt our world position." This statement was an implied criticism anyway. Nevertheless, he agreed with Eisenhower that divisive political statements should not be made "when this country is in trouble." But he did reserve the right as a private citizen to speak out when he had a "constructive alternative course of action."[25] A few days later, speaking in Detroit, Nixon urged a tougher American policy towards the Soviets but only intimated he was unhappy with the Cuban outcome.[26]

During May, Kennedy embraced a program called "Tractors for Freedom," which basically called for trading farm equipment for the refugees who had participated in the Bay of Pigs invasion. Goldwater was adamantly opposed since it was "lending the prestige of the Government to this surrender to blackmail."[27]

Nixon also disagreed with the deal because the U.S. had consistently refused to aid Cuba economically, it would encourage other dictators to take advantage of the United States, and the moral implications of the action were significant since human lives appeared to be items that could be bartered or sold.[28]

Later in the summer, Goldwater delivered a strident speech against the administration's foreign policy. He claimed his speech was designed to counter

an argument for continued drifting in the wrong direction; for inaction on all major cold war fronts; for further costly implementation of an outmoded, weak-kneed foreign policy which accomplishes nothing but more and greater losses of freedom's territory to the forces of international communism.[29]

As viewed from the historical perspective, Republicans were divided during 1961 on their stand over Kennedy's response to Cuba. The top party leaders sought to close ranks and support JFK despite their disagreements over his policies. They also reserved the right to offer constructive alternatives. Congressional voices, on the other hand, were far from soft; rather, their criticism was direct, incisive, and partisan. The hard-line approach from Congress was easy to maintain because the GOP did not have to make the tough choices that it publicly demanded. However, JFK learned from this experience, and his next confrontation with Cuba would be a more severe test. The nation was about to witness a crisis of major proportions, and Republicans offered their support once again as the loyal opposition.

The American wish that Cuba, as a festering point, would fade away was just sheer fantasy. Instead, 1962 brought a more serious confrontation which prompted Republicans to orchestrate their criticism differently. Nixon set the tone for GOP commentary during February. Interviewed on the "Jack Paar Show" from New York City, the former vice president charged that Kennedy should have supplied air support to insure the success of the Bay of Pigs invasion. He further commented "If all the United States does is what the weak and timid will approve, we might as well cash in our chips right now."[30] Two days later, on the same talk show, Rockefeller echoed Nixon's critique. Several weeks later, Goldwater, speaking before the faculty and students at the University of Buffalo, agreed with the criticism of weak logistical support but thought an economic embargo of Cuba by the United States "would be the undoing of Premier Fidel Castro."[31]

Nixon went even further in March when he charged JFK with endangering American security during the 1960 campaign because Kennedy had called for stronger action against Cuba. The irresponsibility, from Nixon's view, was that he knew of Eisenhower's plan to assist training Cuban nationals and of the covert plan for invading the island. Because of Kennedy's claims, Nixon was put in the position of being soft on Castro since he had to disavow the charges so the plan might be protected from disclosure.

There are numerous indications that Republicans—especially congressional leaders—were wary of Kennedy's ability to deal forcefully and effectively with the Soviets. By spring, the tempo of Republican attacks increased. There was a drive to link some Democrats to a so-called plan of surrender. This charge was based on a book called *The Liberal Papers*, which contained articles on

American foreign policy by liberal Democrats. According to published reports in the *New York Times*, Republicans charged that these papers were designed to recognize Communist China, demilitarize West Germany, recognize East Germany, and abandon our missile bases in Europe. Dirksen called the papers our "American Munich," and Halleck was quoted as saying the book proposed "that the United States back out of Asia and Europe with our hands up."[32]

During this same time period, Republicans had been working on their policy statements in preparation for the 1962 and 1964 campaigns. Twelve party leaders from the Senate and House were compiling proposals, and the group was chaired by Congressman Melvin Laird of Wisconsin. The conservative and liberal wings of the party were ostensibly represented by this group, but when the report was finished, several senators voted against it, while the House vote was unanimous. In terms of communism the message was clear: "In foreign policy, the overriding national goal must be victory over Communism through the establishment of a world in which men can live in freedom, security, and national independence. There can be no real peace short of it."[33]

The *New York Times* was critical of Laird's group and wrote an editorial to that effect. Laird's rebuttal came on June 30 in a letter to the editor in which he defended the Republican position and claimed the *Times* had argued against using foreign policy as an issue during the 1962 campaign. Laird further claimed this course of criticism was justified since they were fulfilling their role as the loyal opposition, and his printed rebuttal was as follows:

There are serious differences of opinion about the wisdom of the general course of foreign policy pursued by the present Administration. These doubts have been expressed not only by Republicans, but by Democrats as well. They have been expressed from time to time in the columns of the New York Times. It was not a Republican but your columnist James Reston who called President Kennedy a man who "talked like Churchill and acted like Chamberlain."

But the overriding criterion for deciding when and how to criticize foreign policy must be the national interest in preserving and expanding freedom in the world. To this, all other considerations must give way. Republicans have observed these ground rules in discussing the foreign policy of the Kennedy Administration.

I think the Administration has failed on critical occasions in the past eighteen months to face realistically the fact that communism still seeks the destruction of freedom everywhere. I think that the Administration has failed to act with sufficient vigor to frustrate the achievement of Communist objectives in several instances—particularly in Cuba, Laos, and Berlin.[34]

What all of this did was help set the tone of the fall political races and undoubtedly put extra pressure on the Kennedy administration to maintain a strong stance against communism. There was a feeling among Republicans that Kennedy had to be called to task on his foreign policy. This entire process was setting the stage for that, but its effect would be defused by the Cuban Missile Crisis.

The official Republican view of 1962 echoed many fears about stability of the world order, America's military strength, and our determination or resolve to face the Communist menace. By late June, Halleck was joining Dirksen in responding to matters of domestic and international concern. Halleck zeroed in on the world-wide Communist conspiracy and urged our foreign policy be continued as it had under Eisenhower. "If as we doubt, the Soviets are mellowing," Halleck said, "why change a policy that brought it about? It doesn't make sense. Improvements? Certainly. Basic change? No. Let's keep the policy tough. We must maintain a course of action that is determined and firm."[35] Dirksen continued the barrage during the late summer when he admonished Kennedy for his lack of overall foreign policy. Dirksen was pleased we were standing firm in Berlin, but his skepticism piqued when he thought that JFK was moving towards concessions rather than holding out for principle. About four weeks prior to the midterm congressional elections, Dirksen reiterated the bipartisan approach, but argued, "[T]radition also calls for both political parties to place the facts before the American people prior to a national election, including facts about our posture in the world."[36]

Without a doubt, our posture was in question and the exposed flank was in our backyard, namely Cuba. The administration knew, through public opinion polls, that Cuba was at the forefront of public thought and that Americans wanted the government to do something about the situation. During late August 1962, Republicans argued that the United States was under a direct threat from the Soviets because they had a substantial military commitment to Castro. They played up the threat while the administration tried to defuse the situation by claiming that Castro was in trouble due to the economic boycott; eventually he would be removed from power. Kennedy continued support for covert activities against the regime and tried to hasten the overthrow, but this type of activity could not be publicized. When this was combined with Kennedy's mild public reaction to Republican charges, the president was in a weak position politically as the midterm elections approached.[37]

An event which further exacerbated the condition came when Republican Senator Kenneth Keating (New York) claimed the Russians were shipping offensive missiles to Cuba. He and his fellow Republicans refused to accept the premise that Russian military personnel were on the island only as technicians. The implication was all too clear: Cuba was becoming a Soviet base. In early September, the president had a bipartisan meeting at the White House with congressional leaders and discussed the military buildup in Cuba. The *New York Times* reported that JFK was attempting to stave off heavy Republican criticism since the GOP leaders had announced their intention to make Cuba a campaign issue. Kennedy sought to reassure them that he was following the situation.[38] On the other hand, Barry Goldwater preferred to vent his feelings openly by reiterating his belief in the economic blockade. He hastened to add, "[I]f it takes our military, I wouldn't hesitate to use it. Something must be done about Cuba."[39] Ten days later he characterized Kennedy's policy as "do nothing" and claimed it "virtually promised the Communist world that the United States will take no action to remove the threat of Soviet armed might in the Western Hemisphere."[40]

On September 18, Nixon, not wanting to be left out of the fray, publicly called for a quarantine of Cuba in order to halt the flow of Soviet arms. He pledged his "unqualified support" and said, "Cuba is a cancer," it was the "beachhead" for infiltrating Latin America. When asked about the risk of war, his answer was apocalyptic: "I believe war is risked if Communism is not stopped and is allowed to spread now."[41]

In early October, the Congress passed a joint resolution expressing American resolve to keep Cuba from endangering our security. This resolution had been initiated by Dirksen and Halleck, passed overwhelmingly, and gave a clear feeling on congressional views with this matter. Its importance was to be crucial during the Missile Crisis.

In a book entitled *The Kennedy Crises*, the authors have illustrated how the leading American newspapers had given Keating front-page coverage in September concerning his charges; by October, he received less press and favorable treatment in newspaper editorials. Columnist James Reston of the *New York Times* charged that Keating was not checking his sources with government officials for confirmation. In short, many people thought that Keating was crazy.[42] Amidst all the controversy, a joint session of the Senate Foreign Relations and Armed Services Committees was held in Washington. J. William Fulbright's Latin American expert from the Senate Foreign Relations Committee, Pat Holt, later recalled why the hearings were held:

Keating kept making these charges and everybody got excited as hell about it. The main object of the Joint Hearings, as I recall, was to try to find a formula which would satisfy Keating and the hard liners without doing too much violence to the principle of nonintervention. . . . It was a question of degree, of how tough you got. The question was easy for Keating, Capehart and Goldwater.[43]

The Republican charges, refugees streaming out of Cuba, and the public concern helped the GOP define the Cuban threat. Coupled with Soviet intentions, the problems in the Caribbean became the number-one campaign issue for Republicans. Since the initiative was theirs, they sought to make the most of the situation. Kern has aptly described the public perception of this issue when he wrote, "If the United States could not cope with Castro, ninety miles from Key West, how could it possibly hope to deal with the communist challenge elsewhere?"[44]

Around mid-October, American intelligence sources gathered the first conclusive evidence of Soviet missiles in Cuba. Kennedy announced a quarantine of the island on October 22; Republicans had called for this action weeks before. Republicans had used the issue of Cuba to portray Kennedy as weak, indecisive, or timid, not only in the Caribbean but also with other areas of the world. Even though the GOP had criticized the president when foreign policy was in the formative stages, they demonstrated bipartisanship and closed ranks once the Missile Crisis began.

Eisenhower spoke out on October 22 and took exception with those who would badger Kennedy. In a similar vein, Republican congressional leaders attended a White House meeting where the president outlined the gravity of the situation and explained the measures he had taken. Later, the Republican leaders issued the following statement:

We Republican leaders met today at the White House at the urgent request of the President. We listened to a report of the Central Intelligence Agency, the Secretary of State, and Secretary of Defense; we were told of the unanimous report of the [National] Security Council and the Joint Chiefs of Staff; were informed by the President of his already determined course of action which he later stated in his broadcast for all the world to hear. Americans will support the President on the decision or decisions he makes for the security of our country.[45]

Senator Thomas Kuchel (R-California), Dirksen's whip in the Senate, noted "So far as American foreign policy is concerned, politics has adjourned. This is a deadly serious situation and the American people are going to rally behind the President."[46] The statements at this point almost have a detached character about them. Republicans sat, listened, heard reports, and were made aware of the events transpiring over Cuba. It must be remembered, though, that their input regarding these decisions had been minimal.

On October 23, Eisenhower was still supportive of JFK but also noted the political campaign had to continue. Eisenhower remarked, "[W]e do not have to support him when he speaks or acts as head of a political party; and indeed we do not." He elaborated further by stating, "We are free to ask and to learn how we arrived at our present state, even in foreign affairs." Once the crisis has ended, "it will be entirely proper then to examine and analyze and criticize decisions and actions taken."[47]

Keating, who originally advocated a Cuban quarantine, agreed the issue had to be removed from partisan political debate. He could not understand, though, why he possessed some of the same information the president had obtained weeks before and yet no action had been taken. The only explanation he could find was that the facts were withheld until policy could be developed.[48] However, the senator never revealed his sources. There has been some speculation that his font of information had been from refugee groups who revealed the nature of offensive weapons, their location, and point of origin. Once the confrontation ended, Keating praised Kennedy and offered assurances that Congress was behind him.

Nixon also offered his support for the president. He told a political rally on October 26 that Kennedy had only two choices: inaction or action. If JFK had not acted, Nixon insisted, Castro would have had missiles on his soil. He further theorized, "Khrushchev is not going to risk Moscow to save Havana, but Castro is a madman."[49] Several days later, as tensions eased, Nixon declared that the affair "demonstrates again that when you stand up to Communist aggressors, they back down."[50]

Overall, during 1962 repeated statements concerning the American position relative to the Soviet Union and communism were important reminders issued to Kennedy. The Republican leadership emphasized firm, decisive action when dealing with the Russians. Ironically, Kennedy followed that course during the Cuban Missile Crisis in late October. The perfect political opportunity arose to challenge the president and his party, but the moment never materialized. During those tense days in October, Kennedy sought and received bipartisan support. This was a great credit to men like Dirksen, Halleck, Eisenhower, Nixon, and Rockefeller who put the national interest above party politics.

The problem, of course, was that the congressional leadership (and party leaders) had consistently pressed Kennedy for tough action, and once he took it they were obliged to give support. However, they may have argued behind the scenes that a consistent policy on behalf of the administration might have forestalled any missile crisis. The point is simply this: a political windfall never developed and the GOP still retained a minority position in the Congress with 259 Democrats and 176 Republicans in the House and 68 Democrats and 32 Republicans in the Senate.[51] Hopes for victory were set now on the 1964 presidential race, but matters of international importance were to play a much larger role during the interim.

Beginning in 1963, there was a decided shift in the Republican congressional leadership's response to President Kennedy. Republicans directed their criticism towards him as an individual rather than towards specific agencies or cabinet officers. There was a recurring theme in 1963 and that was to stop Soviet expansion and maintain American military strength. Halleck and Dirksen argued that "one of the major problems in Washington today is discovering what the Kennedy Administration's foreign policy is."[52] The minority leadership was quick to assert that these same questions were being raised within the media and the Democratic party as well. Publicly, Everett Dirksen began to confront the meaning of co-existence between East and West. He wanted substantive actions to demonstrate a willingness of peaceful aims on behalf of Communist nations. The formulation went thus:

Let the Communists give the world some concrete evidence of their desires by a cease-fire and withdrawal in South Vietnam, removal of Soviet troops from Cuba, an end to Communist terror in Venezuela and destruction of the Berlin Wall. It is time the United States made the demands instead of the Soviet Union and won concessions instead of making them.[53]

After the midterm elections, Goldwater, speaking in New York City, delivered a tirade against the administration and urged a purge of the State Department and the removal of United Nations Ambassador Adlai Stevenson and special assistant to the president Arthur Schlesinger, Jr. His reasoning was that this group had "consistently urged a soft policy toward Communism, both in Cuba and elsewhere throughout the world." He also argued that Kennedy's pledge not to invade Cuba "is the greatest victory Communism has won." Goldwater reiterated his faith in Stevenson's loyalty but charged these people did not understand "Communism and the modern world."[54]

Any bipartisan spirit that existed during the Cuban Missile Crisis was short-lived. During 1963, there were numerous attempts to shift the blame for Cuba onto Kennedy's shoulders. Goldwater, looking like an obvious presidential candidate, attacked JFK's foreign policy by saying, "[T]he American Government is worried sick about the new Soviet build-up in Cuba." The charge here was that the president did not want a showdown with the Russians because it would have revealed his mismanagement of the situation.[55] On February 18, the issue of Cuba exploded on Capitol Hill as members of both parties criticized each other; Republicans were especially vicious in their attacks upon the administration. Goldwater demanded a different blockade designed to stop all material from reaching Cuba. Fulbright lashed out at Goldwater, Rockefeller, and Senator Hugh Scott for straying from the bipartisan tradition. But Goldwater retaliated by saying, "[T]he Kennedy Administration wants no part of a bipartisan approach to foreign policy—except when they get into trouble."[56]

Richard Nixon also believed that Kennedy lacked decisiveness since "the Communist cancer from Cuba" had not been eradicated. He pledged bipartisan support for strong actions in the categories of an oil blockade, on-site missile inspections, refusing foreign aid to those nations that traded with Cuba, and removal of Soviet troops. But Nixon was also setting the stage for the 1964 election. He cautioned fellow Republicans that they must "learn to enjoy fighting the Kennedy Administration as much as they seem to enjoy fighting each other." He called for a policy which would "drive Communism from this hemisphere and keep it out of the Americas."[57]

America, of course, had made some demands in the Cuban Missile Crisis, but demanding action in other regions was nearly impossible. Kennedy had faced Republican pressure during his entire term and part of his response to that pressure was action he took in Southeast Asia. Clearly, the GOP wanted something substantial in terms of combating Marxist expansion, and Vietnam became the testing ground for Western and, more importantly, American resolve.

The most enduring foreign policy legacy from Kennedy's tenure came through the increased American commitment to Vietnam. In fact, Southeast Asia was one of his primary concerns during the early 1960s. As a congressman, he had traveled in the area and visited Laos, Cambodia, and Vietnam during 1954. He returned to the United States and was critical of French tactics used to keep Vietnam as part of the colonial empire. According to Arthur Schlesinger, Jr., who was similar to a "historian in residence" during Kennedy's presidency, "The trip gave Kennedy both a new sympathy for the problems of Asia and a new understanding of the power of nationalism in the underdeveloped world."[58] Kennedy foresaw a perilous chain of events within Indochina until France decided to grant Vietnam its independence. But Vietnam was not the most serious problem he faced at the beginning of his presidential term.

One day before leaving the White House, Eisenhower met with his successor and discussed the preoccupation he had over the problem of Laos. Eisenhower believed the takeover there would completely threaten Indochina. He also informed JFK that it would be his responsibility to face the oncoming threat, thereby directly challenging him to follow through on an effective containment for the region. A civil war was raging in Laos, but the new president preferred diplomatic solutions rather than military options which would have put the United States into costly armed ventures. At the same time, Kennedy did not wish to be viewed as the appeaser in relation to Laos. He accepted Eisenhower's domino theory, but the concern went further. As Parmet has observed, "For still another Democrat to yield in Asia, especially in the wake of Eisenhower's creation of the Southeast Asia Treaty Organization (SEATO) with its protective clauses for Indochina, could easily encourage another 'Who lost China?' debate."[59] Kennedy certainly understood that Republicans would lead the charge in this new debate.

During late March 1961, Halleck and Dirksen stated their hope that the United States would not agree to a coalition government in Laos, which included Communists. By the summer of 1962 a cease-fire was arranged and a coalition government created. Eventually, Laos was neutralized and American attention turned towards Vietnam where communism was pitted against democracy.

Kennedy was placed on notice in early 1962 by the joint leadership. They made known their intention to follow the bipartisan tradition enunciated by Vandenberg, but they also gave the president an admonition:

As indicated by our statements, we have never been satisfied with the handling of the Laotian situation; likewise, we have been deeply concerned over Vietnam.

The administration has 1 year of seasoning under its belt. We fully intend to pursue a bipartisan course wherever possible, but it should be made unmistakably clear that when we have sufficient grounds to differ with the President in the best interest of the country, we intend to speak up without hesitation.[60]

By late August they applauded JFK's commitment in Vietnam but expressed unhappiness over the U.S. stance with Communist powers. "By any reasonable standard, the record of the Kennedy administration in foreign affairs has shown lack of understanding, the absence of any overall policy, and a tendency toward concession rather than standing on principle."[61]

The problems in South Vietnam were not going to be solved with a cease-fire or in some other temporary fashion; rather, the turmoil there increased and the American commitment grew as well. Vietnam always had been a curious mix of cultures, subcultures, colonial rule, and diverse religious sects—the most important being Buddhism and Catholicism. Vietnamese leader Ngo Dinh Diem made few improvements within the social and political structure of his nation; eventually this led to his downfall. During 1961, Kennedy faced a series of choices: commit America to an increased military role, maintain the current level of advisory help, or remove the American influence completely. By 1961 there were about two thousand troops—American troops and specialists—stationed in Vietnam. Diem had resisted the presence of American soldiers on his soil because he did not want control of his war with the Communist insurgency shifting to the United States. Furthermore, he continued to refuse the push for internal reforms which Kennedy had consistently urged Diem to accept.[62]

Frances FitzGerald, in her award-winning book *Fire in the Lake*, which details the American involvement in Vietnam as well as the Vietnamese culture, has noted the many-faceted challenges that Diem faced as a leader. His failure to reorganize the economy and social structure of his land led to his eventual demise. Writing of the American economic aid and failure to bring about desired results, FitzGerald has observed:

To pacify the landlords and the businessmen, Diem lowered taxes to almost nothing and put up with the unproductive manorial system of land tenure. The only people who suffered were, of course, the peasants and landless farm laborers; they suffered as they always had under the French from an unjust social system and from the concentration of money in the cities.

Neither the Diem regime nor the Americans could alter their plight, for
a real program of social and economic reform would have involved a real
conflict of interests between the peasants on the one hand and the landlords
and the city people on the other.[63]

Diem chose to believe that the civil war raging in his nation was
being directed on the outside rather than emanating from within.
To view the problem as one of internal factors would have required
serious domestic changes. Kennedy knew what was at stake and
realized that the Communist guerrilla movement was a clever de-
vice aimed at circumventing the traditional defense forces in a nation
by employing the key components of terrorism and political subversion.[64] JFK also grasped the concept that the Vietnamese people
had to be won over if any kind of conflict was to succeed for
freedom's sake. It was not possible to overcome the inherent odds
unless the populace was assured independence at war's end.[65]

By 1963 the ante was up in Vietnam. Kennedy nearly quintupled
the number of American soldiers in Vietnam—less than seven
hundred when he began his term to more than three thousand by
the end of his first year in office—and the number more than tripled
when it reached a high of slightly more than eleven thousand men
by the end of 1962.[66] Now Kennedy was in a quandary. He had
inherited this situation from Eisenhower, was disturbed by Diem's
autocratic style of leadership, and saw the inability of this leader
to relate with the Buddhist elements. The militant government
opposition that led to raids on Buddhist pagodas and self-immo-
lation of their monks only heightened tensions and led to further
alienation. All of these factors brought JFK to the conclusion that
Diem had to be removed. Diem and his brother were murdered in
a coup by the Vietnamese generals on November 1, 1963. Parmet
claims that Kennedy did not want Diem killed and even sent a
personal emissary urging him to seek sanctuary at the American
embassy in Saigon. Diem refused to heed the suggestion. The irony
is that within a few weeks Kennedy was also killed.[67]

The Republican position on Vietnam had been inadequate in
relation to the issues at hand. The usual GOP line was that the
president had to stand firm in response to communism. Southeast
Asia for the minority was just part of a much larger picture which
included areas such as Berlin and Cuba. Cuba especially had grabbed

the headlines and became a preoccupation with the GOP, whether in Congress or as members of the party hierarchy. By 1963, though, several individuals were beginning to speak out about the trouble in Indochina. On April 16, Rockefeller held a news conference in Washington and criticized the president for supporting "freedom fighters" in South Vietnam but not Cuba. He remarked, "I hope it is not as a means or an endeavor to placate or to appease the Soviet."[68] But Kern has noted the irony of the general Republican position; they did not really make Vietnam an issue of great merit. "Republicans did not try to turn his [Kennedy's] difficulties concerning this issue to partisan advantage. Senator Goldwater and others appear to have been waiting quietly for him to make mistakes and then use them against him in the 1964 election."[69] Since Berlin and Cuba captured the headlines, congressional interests and their constituents were relatively quiet. The military commitment to Vietnam was supported by most conservative Republicans; consequently, a political issue never really developed by 1963.

During the fall, and prior to Diem's death, Kennedy wavered between withdrawing American troops and sending more forces to Southeast Asia. He was uncertain about the course the United States was following and he did not want to be caught in another Korea, or facsimile thereof. However, on October 2, the White House announced the removal of one thousand troops by the end of the year. This action was part of a plan to gradually wind the war down.[70] It also was done in anticipation that the war would be over by 1965. A few weeks later Nixon helped clarify his party's position on the war in Vietnam. Speaking in Paris, he said, "I would say that in Vietnam today the choice is not between President [Ngo Dinh] Diem and somebody better, it is between Diem and somebody infinitely worse."[71]

Nixon's comment helps to place the Republican position in some perspective. The GOP had adopted several consistent foreign policy themes by the latter part of 1963. Halting Soviet expansion, maintaining American military strength, and anxiety over Marxist meddling in Cuba or Southeast Asia were all issues the party addressed. Emphasis of party criticism shifted, too. Direct attacks upon JFK by Halleck and Dirksen escalated after 1961 when the Republican leaders advocated that America make demands rather than concessions. Where the political rhetoric began and ended is difficult to determine; the clear premise in this period, though, was a hard-line approach to communism by the loyal opposition. Once again, the irony is that Vietnam was not viewed as a distinct, postcolonial culture and nation. Instead, it became a testing ground for American resolve in the face of Marxist challenges. Republican statements lacked an indication of great depth, or feeling, for the internal dynamics of Vietnam.

John F. Kennedy had made a choice concerning a commitment to aid South Vietnam. This decision was to have profound effects upon the United States, but he left this choice to be handled by his successor, just as Eisenhower had done a few years earlier. The GOP made certain that Kennedy maintained a tough stance against communism and this may have been part of the reason, beyond his own cold war philosophy, for America's presence in Vietnam by late 1963.

1. Senator Arthur Vandenberg (R-Michigan) reviewing his notes before giving a speech to the Senate, 1948. Courtesy: The National Archives.

2. Senator Robert Taft (R-Ohio). Courtesy: The National Archives.

3. President John F. Kennedy throws out the first baseball of the 1963 season. To JFK's right are Postmaster General Larry O'Brien (wearing glasses) and Senator Mike Mansfield (D–Montana); to JFK's left: Senate Minority Leader Everett Dirksen (leaning to side) and House Minority Leader Charles A. Halleck (R-Indiana). Courtesy: The Dirksen Congressional Center.

4. A Republican Leadership Breakfast, August 1965. From left: Rep. Bob Wilson (California), Rep. Les Arends (Illinois), Former President Dwight D. Eisenhower, Rep. Gerald Ford (Michigan), and Rep. Melvin Laird (Wisconsin) standing in the background. Courtesy: The Gerald R. Ford Library.

5. Senator Everett Dirksen congratulates President Lyndon Johnson after his State of the Union Address on January 8, 1964. Courtesy: The Dirksen Congressional Center.

6. House Minority Leader Gerald Ford and Senate Minority Leader Everett Dirksen discuss the question of the week during their "Ev and Jerry Show" on June 9 1966. Courtesy: The Dirksen Congressional Center.

7. House Minority Leader Gerald Ford delivers the Republican State of the Union message, a rebuttal to LBJ, January 19, 1967. Courtesy: The Gerald R. Ford Library.

8. A photo from 1968 showing, from left: Les Arends, Senator Charles Goodell (R-New York), Gerald Ford, and Senator Jacob Javits (R-New York). Courtesy: The Gerald R. Ford Library

9. A Cabinet Room discussion between Johnson, Ford, and Dirksen after a Congressional leadership meeting in January 1968. Courtesy: Lyndon B. Johnson Library.

3.

THE GRAND OLD PARTY DIVIDED

The trauma of John F. Kennedy's assassination rocked the American government to its very foundations. Shock waves sped through the nation as the news poured out of Texas on November 22, 1963. For the first few days the national grief was paralleled with a need to understand America's new president—Lyndon Baines Johnson. Of course, Johnson was faced with an immediate challenge of calming the country after Kennedy's tragic death. This was a task he knew had to be accomplished if the urgent matters—domestic and foreign—were to be handled with dispatch.

Lyndon Johnson was no stranger to the art of politics American style. He began his political career as secretary to a Texas congressman in 1932. He returned to Texas in 1935 as administrator for the National Youth Administration. Two years later, he ran for Congress winning easily in a crowded field of ten people. With his political base secure, Johnson served in the House, then the Senate, and became Jack Kennedy's choice for vice president in 1960. As vice president, he had been thoroughly briefed on matters of state, and Johnson, along with Theodore Sorenson, participated in more high level meetings with the president than any other individual. During 1963 Kennedy decided that Johnson was to be informed about all available contingency plans in case the United States entered nuclear war. All emergency operational and transfer plans of key government personnel had been open to Johnson. As Theodore White has observed, "Because he had participated in all these plans, both panic and ignorance were already precauterized in the Vice-President on the night of November 22, 1963—he knew

exactly all the intricate resources of command and communication
at his disposal."[1]

LBJ entered office with a burden more profound than Kennedy's
assassination; he was plagued during the first few months by the
need to cut a path solely on his own. The Kennedy legacy was his,
as it was the nation's, but he had eleven months to chart a course,
and the ultimate goal was to have a landslide election victory to
offset the narrow win of 1960.[2] Eric Goldman, who was an advisor
to President Johnson for several years, has written about the agenda
during the first few months:

The main effort would go to domestic affairs. While taking every opportunity to dramatize his interest and his competence in foreign affairs, the
new President hoped that he could hold world relations largely in their
existing situation, and above all, that he could avoid crises. Calling upon
the emotions generated by the assassination, using to the hilt his special
relationship to Congress, he would attempt to get the House and Senate
to enact quickly the major legislation proposed by the Kennedy Administration. At the same time, that other prime activity would go ahead—
putting an LBJ stamp on the Administration.[3]

Another source confirms that Johnson was preoccupied with domestic matters and political considerations during his first year in
office; therefore, Secretary of Defense Robert McNamara was allowed to handle the details concerning the American commitment
in Vietnam. A major exception to this pattern occurred during the
late summer of 1964.[4]

There was a moratorium of thirty days in the post-assassination
period as politicians—Republicans and Democrats—accepted the
nonpartisan approach to the political process in deference to Kennedy's memory. However, by January 1964, the curtain began to
rise on Johnson's presidency as he was pressed for answers to questions about foreign and domestic policies. Republicans, uneasy about
the moratorium anyway, and knowing Johnson would seek re-
election, began their assault in late January hoping to defeat the
incumbent during the general election.

As usual, Halleck and Dirksen led the Republican opposition on
Capitol Hill. During January and February 1964, the joint leadership
lashed out at what they claimed was a losing policy within world
affairs. The leadership began by attacking America's foreign policy

stance from a broad perspective and claimed we had a weak foreign policy. Dirksen allowed that NATO was deteriorating, Cuba had gone Communist (a fact already understood in American political circles and no news to anyone), and to make matters worse, Johnson had agreed to a wheat sale with the Soviets. All of these steps had, according to the Senate minority leader, "reduced American prestige," and he further intoned, "It is high time our Government recognized that Communist aggression never stops and never will until we formulate policies to meet the realities presented by a cold, relentless, and inhuman enemy."[5] Interviewed on NBC's "Meet the Press" on February 2, Dirksen conceded that foreign affairs would be a major campaign issue during 1964. He reiterated the domino theory in relation to Vietnam and added further clarification to his position concerning war in Asia:

Well, first I agree that obviously we cannot retreat from our position in Vietnam. I have been out there three times, once as something of an emissary for then President Eisenhower. I took a good look at it. It is a difficult situation, to say the least. But we are in to the tune of some $350 million. I think the last figure I have seen indicates that we have over 15,500 military out there, ostensibly as advisors and that sort of thing. We are not supposed to have combatant troops, even though we were not signatories to the treaty that was signed at Geneva when finally they got that whole business out of the fire. But we are going to have to muddle through for awhile and see what we do. Even though it costs us $1.5 million a day.[6]

Later in February, the joint leadership characterized Johnson's policy on Vietnam as one of vacillation and complained we were adrift with "uncertainty and confusion."[7] By spring, Halleck specifically castigated Johnson with a vacillating policy in Vietnam and further complained that Americans were not being told the truth about our involvement there.[8] In a similar vein, Dirksen said, "Let's have the whole brutal business out on the table and let the American people see it for what it is."[9]

The Republican vexation with the lack of a clearly defined policy at this juncture went even further when Senator Ken Keating demanded a full congressional review of the war in Southeast Asia and America's involvement therein. For Dirksen, though, the inconsistency seemed painfully clear and the outcome for a haphazard

policy was certain to cause future problems. He addressed himself
to that issue on May 25, 1964, during a joint leadership press conference. Dirksen remarked,

If, as is evident, it is difficult for Americans to understand this vacillating
American policy, how demoralizing it must be for the Vietnamese. We
only know that indecision in Washington is dribbling away both American
lives and American prestige in Southeast Asia. We think the time has come
for President Johnson to announce a firm policy and pursue it with vigor.[10]

Criticism of Johnson's Vietnam policy was emanating from areas
other than Republican circles on Capitol Hill; a groundswell of
opposition was rising up on the campaign trail. The spring primary
season was well under way during 1964 as Republicans questioned
Johnson's methodology and strength of purpose in Asia. By March,
Republican candidates and party leaders were crisscrossing the nation in an attempt to arouse the voters and enlist people to their
cause; a cause, if one took it literally, designed to save the Republic
from impending disaster.

Key party leaders began the assault on Johnson and the Democrats
in late January. Thomas E. Dewey, himself a two-time presidential
candidate, assailed the Democrats during a speech in Philadelphia.
He charged them with failing to remove Castro from Cuba and
noted, "[W]e have been successfully insulted, humiliated and held
up to scorn in Zanzibar, Cambodia, Vietnam and Panama." He
further stated:

We ought to pull up our socks and act like responsible, intelligent Americans again. We have the great nuclear and missile power which the Republicans built up. It is time we recovered our sense of purpose, our skill
and our courage in using our brains and our power to preserve the peace.
   The tragedies of the last three years have resulted from basic confusions
and weaknesses in the Democratic party. It has always had deep ideological
splits within itself, which show up most painfully in the explosive and
dangerous field of foreign affairs.[11]

Nixon was also part of the fight. Speaking in Peoria, Illinois, on
February 22, 1964, he claimed Johnson was preparing for defeat or
retreat in Vietnam and this would eventually allow communism to
capture the entire area.[12] By April, he judged the stakes over Viet-

nam to be even higher, because war in that country was only part of the entire problem in Southeast Asia. He felt the conflict might have to be extended into Laos and North Vietnam for purposes of "hot pursuit" in order to follow fleeing Communist forces from Vietnam as they sought sanctuary in neighboring territories.[13] His most damning declaration, however, came during a speech in early May when he argued that "respect and trust in United States leadership is now at its lowest point in Asia since World War II."[14]

Another party and congressional leader was Melvin Laird of Wisconsin who, in a little-noticed news item from Washington, claimed that Johnson was preparing to strike into North Vietnam. Laird would not reveal his source or whether military action was imminent; he just stated his belief. Ironically, Johnson did order air strikes into North Vietnam the following year. In the same news story Senator George Aiken, Republican from Vermont, commented on the possibility of an expanded war and his remark was nothing short of prophetic.

If we went into this area where people are not asking us, where they don't want war, where they are still getting along peacefully today, then it would be a major error. . . . I think we've made about every mistake in the book in Southeast Asia.[15]

Men such as Laird, Aiken, or even Nixon were not to become presidential contenders during 1964. Instead, two other politicians moved to the forefront and wrestled for the Republican nomination; Barry Goldwater and Nelson Rockefeller were destined to battle for the top spot on the ticket. Their contest had serious ramifications for the GOP, but the rift within their ranks had been building for some time. Even during Kennedy's administration, speculation ran anew over who would lead the opposition during 1964. Nixon, branded a loser, was out of favor with many party regulars. But this was not the central problem; philosophy was to be the watchword for this race.

For years, Republicans had campaigned on the concepts of less government and less spending. Author Theodore White explained the difference between Democrats and Republicans in a unique way when he wrote, "Republicans are for virtue, the Democrats for Santa Claus."[16] The issue went much further, however. The ongoing problem between conservative and liberal wings in the Republican party could be traced back prior to World War II. Ironically, though the GOP had accepted political responsibility by backing strong defense measures and the interstate system in the postwar period, Republicans never campaigned on these major accomplishments. Instead, their posture was essentially to criticize domestic expenditures.

Although the two final contenders for the Republican nomination had some fundamental similarities over a strong national defense and balanced budgets, their personal backgrounds represented stark contrasts.

Diversity was a key component of Nelson Rockefeller's character. He had a keen interest in virtually every matter, possessed tremendous physical energy, and had been exposed to politics most of his adult life. Financial security had surrounded him since birth. He was not only the beneficiary of inherited wealth, he had received a name synonymous with American industrial and financial power. Rockefeller favored American participation with the United Nations, supported Kennedy's Nuclear Test Ban Treaty, liked Medicare for the elderly, and had distributed extra aid to education while governor of New York. All of these factors complicated Rockefeller's quest for the opportunity to lead his party in November; however, there was another issue that clouded his political ambitions. The governor's divorce and subsequent remarriage to a woman named Happy changed the public perception of this man. It was an especially painful situation since the new Mrs. Rockefeller did not have custody of her children from her first marriage. In the very narrow view of some, it seemed as if a mother had deserted her children. The name, the political record, and the personal life complicated the candidacy of an energetic man for the nation's highest office.[17] One of Rockefeller's biographers has written about the problems he had as a Republican:

His sophisticated social concerns, his chic eastern internationalism, his grandiose visions and grand spending did not set well with those Republicans who knew what it was to sweat out a bear market. . . . A more plausible explanation for his failure is that Nelson Rockefeller was in the wrong party.[18]

Barry Goldwater was the titular leader of a group that felt betrayed by the sellout that had transpired when Nixon and Rockefeller agreed to the Compact of Fifth Avenue in 1960. This agreement had bridged some differences within Republican philosophy and helped solidify Nixon's hold on the nomination that year. Goldwater was born in Arizona, went into the family's department store business, became a pilot in the Air Force during World War II, and then returned home to Phoenix and led a crusade to rid the city of vice and corruption. For Goldwater, the frontier still possessed simple virtues. The American ethic of hard work and frugality brought rewards to those who were in business, or at least followed the credo. In this setting, the individual was central to his philosophy; issues were clear cut and very little gray entered the scene.[19]

First elected to the United States Senate in 1952, Goldwater compiled a conservative record in fiscal matters and foreign affairs. His conservatism, though, was more than a matter of public policy; Goldwater found a constituency, or they found him, of decent people who were unsure of the changes that were occurring within American society. Theodore White has perceptively described the inherent characteristics of this constituency:

What is valid of the old morality and what is not? Across the country, from Maine to California, families and individuals, cherishing the old virtues and seeing them destroyed or ignored or flouted, were in ferment. Across the sky of politics there began to flow new names like the John Birch Society, the Minutemen, the National Indignation Convention, Freedom-in-Action and other groups. At the extreme of the frustration were madmen and psychopaths disturbed by conspiracy, Negroes, Jews, Catholics, beardies, but toward the center of it involved hundreds of thousands of intensely moral people who hated and despised not only adultery but Communism, waste, weakness, government bureaucracy, and anarchy.[20]

Even though Goldwater and Rockefeller came from distinct backgrounds and had dissimilar political philosophies, their views on communism were strikingly close. In his book *Where I Stand*, Goldwater wrote about Vietnam and the Communist menace. He said, "It is a major battlefield of the free-world struggle against the Communist threat to engulf all of free Asia. And our allies, in Europe as well as in Asia, ought to be supporting our efforts."[21] Goldwater did not counsel withdrawal of American support from

Vietnam; on the contrary, he believed we had to keep the people and resources of that area from falling into Marxist hands. Therefore, America must have the goal and desire to win the war. Goldwater had strongly urged military intervention in Vietnam during 1963. His views during the 1964 campaign remained the same; the only distinction he made was with methodology in the military tactics.

Goldwater was fond of comparing defeat in Asia with Korea. During a spring primary swing through California, he charged that Americans were facing another Korea-type war. He noted that a loss in Vietnam "will be a far more costly loss than the humiliating defeat we have suffered in Korea. It will mean the loss of the whole of Southeast Asia." Goldwater chided Johnson for not wanting to win, and he observed, "[H]e only says we will contain them."[22] Any stalemate in Vietnam, according to the Arizona senator, was to be "placed squarely in the laps of those twin commanders of chaos, Lyndon B. Johnson and Robert S. McNamara."[23] Part of Goldwater's primary campaign strategy was to argue that a Republican victory in the fall also would bring a victory in Vietnam because he would aggressively prosecute the conflict. A very controversial situation developed when Goldwater publicly *theorized* that "low yield" atomic weapons could be used in Vietnam to defoliate the vegetation, thereby exposing the supply lines into the south. A spokesman for Goldwater later claimed this was only a contingency plan, one not necessarily advocated by the candidate, but the media picked up on the idea and he became branded as an extremist.[24] Goldwater did take a resolute stand, however, when he said he would institute a "win policy" for South Vietnam. His instructions to military commanders would be, "that it was their problem and to get on with solving it."[25]

Rockefeller's general position on Marxism was akin to Goldwater's notions. The New York governor was once questioned about his views on Vietnam and communism in general. One of his biographers has written that both issues merited his serious attention:

But Nelson's inner convictions were unambiguous—he was a hawk in full feather. He approached Vietnam with simplistic certainty. American democracy had provided the soil for the rise of the Rockefellers, who in turn had enriched their country, he believed, almost as much as America had enriched them. Communism was a moral threat to the system that had blessed his family and his country. The Vietnam war was being fought to stop Communism and to maintain America's world primacy; therefore, it was a just war.[26]

Rockefeller had enlightened himself on communism prior to World War II. He had read *Das Kapital*, in which Marx had spelled out the entire struggle. His discovery was shocking and "he spoke with wide-eyed earnestness of someone who had just discovered sin."[27]

During the early campaign of 1964 he denounced Johnson's "double talk" on South Vietnam. Rockefeller charged that the entire area was threatened by communism and sought a "full accounting" of the area.[28] He agreed with Goldwater that the loss of South Vietnam would leave the balance of Southeast Asia in jeopardy, but in late February he claimed that "news management by the Administration has kept the hard facts of the military action from the American people."[29] In late April, he gave "unswerving" support for air attacks by the South Vietnamese against supply lines from Laos and North Vietnam. Essentially, he advocated a wider war, especially by South Vietnamese forces, but his tough anticommunist rhetoric was unmistakable.[30]

Rockefeller supported Goldwater's contention that South Vietnamese forces had to follow the concept of hot pursuit in order to quell the Communist attacks from neighboring areas. In Rockefeller's judgment, the communists were to be warned that "we will bomb their supply lines and bases." There was a fine distinction, though, between the use of American air power and South Vietnam's air force. But the issue for Rockefeller was clear cut: move to win the war by military means.[31]

The summer of 1964 was to be a fateful time for the American commitment to Asia; it was also a crucial period for the Republican party. The GOP grabbed center stage in the media during the week of July 13 as their national convention opened in San Francisco. Despite preliminary challenges from Pennsylvania Governor William Scranton, Henry Cabot Lodge, Michigan Governor George Romney, and Rockefeller, the presidential nomination went to Goldwater. The stage was then set for major changes in the Republican platform. Conservatives had won their battle for leadership of the GOP; moderate and liberal wings of the party were cast aside causing resentment in many quarters. Although the foreign policy section of the platform was similar in length to its 1960 predecessor, the tone had changed dramatically in four years. The plank on international relations was entitled "Failures of Foreign Policy" and began with the following preface: "This Democratic Administration has been, from its beginning, not the master but the prisoner of major events. The will and dependability of its leadership, even for the defense of the free world, have come to be questioned in every area of the globe."[32] The plank further indicted Democrats for a variety of deficiencies, especially in Southeast Asia and Vietnam. The platform charged the Johnson administration with the following errors:

It has abetted further Communist takeover in Laos, weakly accepted Communist violation of the Geneva Agreement, which this present Administration perpetrated, and increased Soviet influence in Southeast Asia.

It has encouraged an increase of aggression in South Vietnam by appearing to set limits on America's willingness to act—and then, in the deepening struggle, it has sacrificed the lives of Americans and allied fighting men by denial of modern equipment.[33]

On the last evening of the convention, Goldwater continued the vilification of Democratic foreign policy in his acceptance speech. He called for high moral leadership—a crusade, if you will—to attack the evils of the day. He declared war on moral decadence, aimless youth, violence in the streets, and communism as the evil incarnate. But his recurring theme was one of failure as demonstrated through examples and analogies:

[F]ailures cement the wall of shame in Berlin. Failures blot the sands of shame at the Bay of Pigs. Failures mark the slow death of freedom in Laos. Failures infest the jungles of Vietnam.

Yesterday it was Korea. Tonite it is Vietnam. Make no bones of this. Don't try to sweep this under the rug. We are at war in Vietnam. [Applause] And yet the President, who is Commander-in-Chief of our forces, refuses to say—refuses to say, mind you, whether or not the objective over there is victory. And his Secretary of Defense continues to mislead and misinform the American people, and enough of it has gone by.[34]

The lines of demarcation had been drawn and Goldwater intended to make this a philosophical campaign, one based on a conservative morality designed to save America. In terms of foreign policy, the themes were consistent: clear enunciation of Southeast Asia policy and, of course, victory in Vietnam. Theodore White has characterized the ideological dedication as a crusade and it was a movement which profoundly affected conservatives.

Thus Goldwater was left, from beginning to the end of the Republican civil war of 1964, in command of the high moral ground. The fervor, the frenzy and the excesses of the dedicated Goldwater troops appalled a huge and unknowable percentage of Republicans of other moralities; but there was no banner to which they could commit themselves. And so Goldwater and his Puritans were left alone to face the greatest pragmatist of all time— Lyndon B. Johnson.[35]

If July was a decisive month for the direction of the Republican party, the events of August were even more dramatic for Lyndon Johnson and the nation's commitment to Vietnam. Prior to August, the major conservative complaint about our Vietnam stance was either poor strategic military policy, improper use of funds for foreign policy, or a weakness in our military posture. Given this backdrop the stage was set for a major shift in America's plan of action and it was one to which Republicans would harken.

THE GULF OF TONKIN

American destiny has always been moved by numerous events beyond American control. However, when United States warships are attacked the nation's full attention is focused on the incident. And so it was during the early morning hours of August 2, 1964, when the destroyer USS *Maddox* was reportedly attacked in the Gulf of Tonkin, which lies east of North Vietnam. The *Maddox* was on routine intelligence patrol in the area when North Vietnamese PT boats began closing in on her. She later opened fire on the boats and sank one. After the incident, the destroyer rendezvoused with another American destroyer, the USS *Turner Joy*. Although the *Maddox* sustained no damage or casualties, the entire event came as a "surprise" to the Johnson administration. Several

members of Congress were briefed about the incident and Dirksen
was one of them. Even though the Illinois senator had been a
frequent critic of our Southeast Asian policy, he saw this first attack
as "one more item in the Communist bag of tricks."[36] At the same
time, however, he called for a further examination of our role there
and the rising financial commitment.

There was a second confrontation with North Vietnamese vessels
on the night of August 4 and this time both the *Turner Joy* and the
Maddox were involved. Radar screens indicated that there were
foreign objects near the American ships, but numerous salvos and
strafing from air support uncovered nothing. There were suppos-
edly torpedo launchings from enemy ships. However, no damage
was sustained by American warships. The details of this second
incident were sent to Washington. Early on, Johnson had exercised
restraint, but he swung around to the view held by his military
advisors that retaliation upon North Vietnam was not only warranted but essential. Although Johnson had decided to use the term
"limited response," Dirksen argued this action was too soft.[37]

The bombing raids launched against North Vietnam for retaliation were directed towards military installations and supply de-
pots. Johnson, though, sought more assurance from Congress.
Therefore, a resolution outlining congressional support was drawn
up for approval on Capitol Hill. The resolution gave Johnson jus-
tification for increased military action which the public needed if
matters went further. A premise was also created by the administration that if we failed to intervene then our commitment to
South Vietnam had been breached. Intervention, and the ensuing
escalation, became a moral and legal obligation of the nation.[38]

The Tonkin Gulf Resolution, as it became known in American
history, easily passed through Congress during August. Senator J.
William Fulbright, Arkansas Democrat and chairman of the Foreign
Relations Committee, pushed the resolution through the Senate.
Ironically, Fulbright became one of the most articulate and ardent
critics of the Vietnam War when he saw the inherent abuses of
administration actions years later. Republicans, for the most part,
were supportive of the measure. Questions concerning the resolution's breadth were raised by Republican Senator John Sherman
Cooper of Kentucky. Cooper's reservations centered around the
scope of presidential power and its exercise therein. Fulbright sug-

gested there was no real limit. A portion of their exchange on the Senate floor is worth noting:

Cooper: In other words, we are now giving the President advance authority to take whatever action he may deem necessary? . . .

Fulbright: I think that is correct.

Cooper: Then, looking ahead, if the President decided that it was necessary to use such force as could lead into war, we will give that authority by this resolution?

Fulbright: That is the way I would interpret it.[39]

The House vote was unanimous while only two senators objected to the resolution. Democrats Wayne Morse of Oregon and Ernest Gruening of Alaska voted against the resolution. The Tonkin Gulf Resolution was not without precedent in American history. The Formosa Resolution, the Cuban Resolution, and the Cuban Missile Crisis were all occasions of national emergency; therefore, Johnson's request was not unusual. The Senate was cursory in its examination of Johnson's resolution and one reason for that may have been that they trusted him. He still had many friends there; he had been one of their own. They did not consider the possibility that he might mislead them, but more importantly they never envisioned that approval of the resolution gave the administration an imprimatur for redirecting America's relationship towards Vietnam.[40] The resolution, though, may have had a deterrence value. Simply stated, a military response by the United States was viewed as a way of deterring North Vietnam from sending increased aid to the South. Since the resolution was not thoroughly discussed on the Senate floor, it may have been understood that the resolution needed no further elaboration.[41]

Although Johnson did not proceed with a major escalation of the war until after the November election, he considered numerous options during the interim. From all indications, McGeorge Bundy, national security advisor to the president, offered LBJ three alternatives: (1) have a full-scale war as in Korea; (2) withdraw; (3) continue the present course with increasing support for South Vietnam.[42] Johnson decided to accept the last option but did widen the scope of the war and America's involvement after the election.

It is not surprising that Republicans were primarily supportive of the resolution and Johnson's subsequent actions. His actions were akin to a strategy, or position, they had long advocated. This entire situation, however, did shift the emphasis to Johnson, put the issue of Vietnam under his control, and removed a key political point which could have been developed by Goldwater. Hubert Humphrey, Johnson's running mate in 1964, referred to the political shift for the near future—and presumably the following year— when he wrote Johnson that 1965 would be "the first year when we can face the Vietnam problem without being preoccupied with the political repercussions from the Republican right."[43].

In early August, Goldwater dutifully announced his support of the president's actions when he stated, "[W]e cannot allow the American flag to be shot at anywhere on earth if we are to retain our respect and prestige. . . . I believe it is the only thing that he can do under the circumstances."[44] Later, Goldwater's responses reverted to the traditional mode of a political campaign. He blasted Johnson on his foreign policy and urged full disclosure of U.S. policy towards Vietnam. As early as April 1964, LBJ had offered Republican candidates national security briefings and classified materials so they might have more depth when it came to foreign policy discussions. Arthur Krock, writing in a *New York Times* editorial, suggested that the president's offer did nothing more than hamper the opposition party since its candidates would be inhibited when discussing classified material for fear of breaching national security. "Responsible discussion of foreign policy," Krock wrote, "which is the President's stated objective of his offer, can be made by competent analysis of the public record, since the policies, or their lack are self-evident."[45]

Unfortunately for Republicans, and their candidate, Johnson held the momentum on Vietnam. Philosophically, most members of the GOP's leadership and congressional ranks supported the war. Goldwater was relegated to making charges against his opponent during the fall campaign and really offered no alternative policy for Vietnam. He claimed in late September that Johnson had lied to the American people about the war, but he never specified his charges.[46] Goldwater's philosophical preoccupation with the Communist threat was readily apparent as he spoke before the American Legion Convention in Dallas on September 23, 1964. His remarks were reminiscent of the convention in San Francisco:

Now, the great, harsh fact of today's troubled world is that Communism is at war; and it's at war against us, at war against all non-Communist nations. The great, harsh fact is that Communism wants the whole world. In Cuba, in the Congo, at the Berlin Wall, in Indonesia, in Vietnam—wherever the flames of conflict are being fanned, Communism is the cause.

Now, the methods it uses in its unrelenting drive to conquer the world are based solely upon expediency. What Communism will do, how far it will go, at any given moment, depends upon their hardheaded, cold-blooded assessment of the risks that they must face.

If they can bury us, as they've promised to do—if they can win the world, as they've said they will—if they can do this without nuclear war, then they will try to avoid nuclear war. But remember this: It is not compassion or decency which prevents their attacking us. It's not concern for our children. It's just plain fear. They respect our power and they fear its use against them.[47]

A week later, Goldwater charged LBJ with being "soft on communism." According to news reports, this was the first time he had used the phrase in reference to the president, and he repeated it four times. He also claimed that "drift, deception, and defeat" were maxims of this administration.[48] Several days later when the senator was questioned about a Republican strategy, or answer on the fight with communism, he said there was "no easy solution." When pressed about Johnson's supposed softness on communism, he claimed it had been a campaign issue that had run through the entire season. Goldwater also noted this idea was Nixon's and Herbert Hoover's and Goldwater was following through with it in his campaign to see the public reaction.[49]

The Republican nominee tried to gain the upper hand in early October by advocating that Eisenhower lead a mission to Vietnam should he win the White House. The president-elect would then have first-hand information on what was happening in that war-torn nation. Press reports indicated this proposal had not been discussed, nor cleared through Eisenhower; however, he had been informed of Goldwater's statement before it became public knowledge. The former general responded to the proposal in a cautious way, citing his age and the responsibility such a mission would entail, but he would have to discuss the matter personally with Goldwater should he win the White House.[50]

Johnson, falling back on one of his favorite ploys, said he was only trying to carry out Eisenhower's policies. He further neutralized the situation when he noted that a Republican (Henry Cabot Lodge) was our ambassador to Saigon.[51] At this juncture it would be an understatement to say that LBJ had stolen Goldwater's thunder. Here was a Republican presidential candidate charging the incumbent with being soft on communism, drawing Eisenhower into the battle, and Johnson countered him every step of the way.

As the election drew closer, Goldwater's remarks became more shrill. Speaking in Maryland he said, "Lyndon Baines Johnson has sowed the wind of weakness. . . . He has reaped the whirlwind of war." Goldwater claimed another word could have been substituted for a feeble response to Marxism and someone from the audience cried "treason!" Goldwater's response was, "That's it."[52] He continued the vilification of his Democratic opponent when he said, "They have never stopped deceiving the American public and the free world. American sons and grandsons are being killed by Communist bullets and Communist bombs. And we have yet to hear a word of truth about why they are dying."[53]

Nixon campaigned for the GOP ticket during the fall. While stumping Maine, he remarked that Johnson was preparing "for action after this election in Vietnam." His information indicated that a withdrawal of the American presence or approval of a coalition government was being considered. In Nixon's judgment, "respect for America is at an all-time low." The only obvious answer, then, was that Goldwater's election to the White House could restore American credibility.[54] Goldwater picked up this theme of America's international position and twisted the matter further. He knew Johnson was not a Communist, nor were the Democrats, "but the Communists have made greater strides when the Democratic party has been in than when the Republican party is in."[55] In his final campaign speech, he placed the issue squarely before the voters and noted that communism was the only great threat to peace. According the Goldwater, "The Republican party is the peace party. We are the peace party because we understand the enemy. We understand his aims. We understand that he always has and always will take risks and seek advantages when tempted by weakness."[56]

The electorate, however, was unmoved by the Republican crusade. Goldwater's call for a change of direction and new leadership fell on deaf ears. When the votes were tallied, he held about 38 percent of the popular vote and carried only six states. In Congress, the portents of the Republican defeat were tremendous. The GOP lost three Senate seats and forty in the House. This defeat painfully reinforced the Republican position as the party out of power; it also allowed the administration to continue its policy in Vietnam which eventually led to military escalation. Many Republicans welcomed the vigorous commitment but eventually the war became a nightmare for the politicians and the people.

CHALLENGE TO THE OLD GUARD

Barry Goldwater's defeat was indicative of a much wider set of problems within Republican ranks. It was troublesome enough that he offered no alternative to Johnson's Vietnam policy; his agreement with the objective was understandable because he wanted a winning policy. But he never captured the hearts and minds of the voters. The issue, essentially, was one of image; not only Goldwater personally but the Republican party generally. Kennedy had entered the presidency with vigor, youth, and at least a semblance of ideas that were forward looking; Johnson inherited this tradition and tried to build upon it. The Republican cast of politicians appeared obstructionist to these ideas; in some cases they were reactionary. Goldwater's philosophy was not the only problem that troubled younger Republicans; it was the image projected to the voters.

Rumors began to circulate as early as August 1964 that Charlie Halleck was going to face a challenge as minority leader, and eventually these rumors became public knowledge. The dissatisfaction stemmed from his lack of constructive alternatives to Democratic programs and an alleged failure to allow younger Republicans to help formulate party policy.[57] The first hints of trouble began in 1963 when Gerald R. Ford of Michigan was elected chairman of the conference. Ford represented some of the new blood which was about to enter key leadership posts for the GOP on Capitol Hill. His selection as chairman became a harbinger for future challenges to the old guard.

After Goldwater's trouncing at the polls, shock waves hit Congress. Representatives such as Mel Laird and Ford called for Republican unity to heal the party but other congressmen, such as

Charles Goodell of New York and Robert Griffin of Michigan, were bent on a move to oppose Halleck. Activists and energetic Republicans like Laird, Goodell, and Griffin were able to persuade a majority of their colleagues that if the GOP was ever to achieve majority status in Congress, it needed a leader who projected a stronger public image, a person who would set the stage for alternative programs to Johnson's proposals.[58]

Halleck was vulnerable for other reasons. The loss of forty seats in November 1964 removed some of his supportive power base. There was also some rancor over a previous fight for minority leader when the Indiana Republican ousted Joseph Martin in 1959. Finally, several of the loyal conservatives were dismayed when Halleck joined forces, first with Kennedy and then Johnson and Dirksen, to pass the Civil Rights Act of 1964.[59] Consequently, the way was cleared for a direct challenge.

The Republican conference held a meeting on December 14 to discuss changes within their leadership. Even though Ford presided at this meeting, no direct challenge to Halleck was made. The Griffin-Goodell team still believed Halleck could not survive a direct assault, and they convinced Ford to seek the minority leader's post. He agreed, making a formal announcement for his bid on December 18. Halleck, in turn, organized his forces in order to defeat Ford, but the effort was futile. One of Halleck's biographers has written, "It was clear from the outset of the Halleck-Ford fight that the struggle was not over conflicting ideologies. It was a battle of personalities, leadership techniques, and style. The two contestants had almost identical voting records."[60] The conference met again on January 4, 1965; Ford replaced Halleck and Laird was chosen as the new chairman. This struggle for succession did not affect all policy-making positions, but the significant changes were now complete at the top. The importance of these House battles, though, was that they represented a much larger picture; the process for reorganization and renewal of the Republican party was underway.

REPUBLICAN RENEWAL, REORGANIZATION, AND REDIRECTION

The overwhelming Republican defeat of 1964 was felt in many areas of the party hierarchy. As the GOP tried to reorganize itself, they faced a fateful choice: how could their image be changed to reflect the 1960s and beyond? Even more crucial was the need to expand the party's base, attract new voters, and plan for elections in the future. The issues, principles, and choices were not easy but two consecutive defeats for the White House had a debilitating effect upon morale, as well as the national image. The defeat of 1964 had been, by all standards, the worst since the days of FDR; therefore, the situation demanded choices and new alternatives. The changes had manifested themselves in two ways: the first within the congressional leadership; the second within the party's personnel structure and creation of the Republican Coordinating Committee.

As we have seen already, the changes on Capitol Hill, at least within the House, were fairly widespread. A new group of younger, innovative, and savvy politicians was moving to the forefront. Their names would be part of America's political scene for many years into the future. Gerald Ford, the University of Michigan football player, Yale law graduate, and congressman from Grand Rapids, Michigan, became the minority leader. At the time, his highest ambition was to be Speaker of the House, but in 1974 he would become president of the United States.

Melvin Laird, congressman from Wisconsin, came from a well-to-do family with timber and logging interests in his home state. At least one colleague has called him "the idea man" and one of the most formidable of the seated members because of the innovative approaches he took towards the problems.[61] Laird became chairman of the conference and a few years later was named secretary of defense under Richard Nixon.

Another innovator was Congressman Charles Goodell of New York. Goodell, who also had a law degree from Yale, entered Congress in 1959 after winning a special election to fill a vacancy in his district. Because of his intellect, Richard Nixon had dubbed him the "egghead of the Republican party."[62] Goodell had been an early backer of Ford and helped maneuver him into the chairmanship of the conference in 1963. Goodell and Laird helped engineer Halleck's defeat in early 1965. Goodell would later move to the Senate in 1968 in order to fulfill the unexpired term of New York's assassinated senator, Robert F. Kennedy. By the late 1960s Goodell also would move to disengage the United States from Vietnam by sponsoring a bill in the Senate designed to cut off appropriations for the war one year after his bill was introduced.

These men became the genesis of a reform movement within the House of Representatives. But their minority status had increased as of 1965, and they were deeply frustrated. Republicans also needed alternatives to the Democrats because they were constantly on the defensive. Goodell, in an interview, remarked about this frustration and the quest for innovation:

[It] was probably best symbolized during that period by the Ev and Charlie Show. Charlie Halleck was the straight man for Ev Dirksen on television, on weekly press conferences, and it frustated the hell out of a lot of us who were young and at that point thought we could change the world a little bit and here these guys were going on with the same routine.[63]

But for Goodell the issue was even more profound. Besides the image, it was an attitudinal problem, one enhanced by a psychological position.

Republicans had a minority psychology [because they] came out of the depression years, and the years of Roosevelt and Truman's domination of the Democratic Party in national politics. The minority psychology tended to be very very negative. We did not, in those days, have the single issue phenomenon . . . in proportion to today. . . . The conservatives in the Republican party have a great deal in common with conservatives in the southern wing of the Democratic party on foreign policy and on a variety of domestic issues.[64]

Consequently, Republicans were usually responding, in concurrence with southern Democrats, to policy rather than gathering up innovative ideas and opposing the Democratic initiatives. In a sense, they lacked force, but realistically they were hampered because of their minority political position.

The new leadership team—Ford, Laird, Goodell, and others—was destined to lead the party through some very turbulent times. Fortunately, their feelings on the loyal opposition ran in a similar vein. Each believed the loyal opposition was obligated, as Gerald Ford has said, to offer "in selected areas, vigorous challenges to the validity of the majority party's policies [and] programs. It involves also the presentation of alternatives, or options."[65] Laird has gone even further to suggest that it is necessary to have debate and dialogue, making your position known early before decisions are made; however, you must have "full and total access to the decision-making process." As far as LBJ was concerned, Laird has said he allowed "no opportunity for the loyal opposition to be taken into consideration on the takeoff of many decisions. We were always expected to be there for the landing, though."[66]

Goodell has argued that there is a clear distinction in time of war or national emergency when you support the president. Since he is the commander in chief, Congress normally will give its support. This was especially true before Vietnam, which was apparently the watershed for this feeling since the commitment was so different. Goodell claims Korea began the process of eroding support and U.S. commitment in Southeast Asia shattered it because of the length of the war. The problem was exacerbated further with suspicion on the part of the public and the Congress concerning the president's foreign policy goals.

However, in the domestic arena the fight continued without abatement.[67] Philosophy aside, practical politics has been, and always will be, part of Washington or any governmental center. On Capitol Hill, at least, by 1965 the leadership team comprised Dirksen in the Senate and Ford in the House. These men were supplemented by others such as Laird, Goodell, and Arizona Congressman John Rhodes on the House Policy Committee. The whip in the Senate was Thomas Kuchel of California, and Margaret Chase Smith of Maine served as chairman of the conference.

With an organized team several other factors had to be considered, not the least of which was the public's perception of this group and its organizational ability. Goodell has ranked Mel Laird with men like Johnson, Nixon, and Dirksen in terms of political acumen.

Mel Laird always knew where the sources of power were, and he ran circles around Jerry Ford as a politician—internal politician, I mean figuring out who decides who gets hired, how money is spent. . . . He took the conference chairmanship from a position of inconsequence to the second most powerful position in the House. . . . He knew how to get all the appointments made by the conference chairman and the conference is the central organizing group for Republicans.

But organizational skill is only one facet of politics. Public image is also necessary to garner a following, and Ford had the desirable

traits. Again, Goodell commented, "Jerry was much better publicly, a nice guy, honest, and straight forward and so forth."[68]

Ford viewed his new role as minority leader in a constructive
way. He believed that Republicans favored the joint leadership
position, but they also wanted a "unified and more aggressive Republican leadership."[69] Hence, the GOP leadership on Capitol Hill
adopted a new stance, one of change and new directions. But Lyndon Johnson was still in the White House and his position required
some maneuvering on behalf of the minority.

Two views have emerged on the Johnson leadership style during
this time period. Gerald Ford notes he and LBJ had major differences on domestic policy. The Republican goal of a free Vietnam
was in harmony with the administration; the differences occurred
especially over the conduct of war in Vietnam. Ford characterized
Johnson as "hard driving," "tough," with "a few rough edges."
All this aside, Ford claims they had a "good working relationship,"
even though Johnson would make some derogatory comments—
usually political rhetoric—but they never bothered the minority
leader. Ford has stressed the point that Johnson "ran the show."
His secretary of state, Dean Rusk, would be present at meetings
or hearings to "smooth over some of the . . . positions that Lyndon
took." However, Dirksen and Ford would tell LBJ how they felt
about issues and he would hear them out. "I think he respected
our position," Ford has said, " . . . and I think he did incorporate
it in his decision making."[70] Laird has been more critical of Johnson
by claiming the president would not give an agenda to leaders for
leadership meetings when it came to areas of foreign policy. Laird
refused to be used in this process and told Johnson, at least via a
letter, that he would not attend these meetings unless agendas were
provided.[71]

Even though the reins of leadership changed within the House
during early 1965, a new organization was developed which paralleled the change while accentuating a different response in the
area of policy alternatives. Obviously, an area of rising concern
was the United States policy in Southeast Asia. From early 1965
on, Ford had no difficulty developing a consensus in the House on
Vietnam. There was, according to the former minority leader, "a
high degree of unity . . . on both sides of the aisle including Republicans on what we were basically seeking to achieve in Viet-

nam."[72] Laird, though, was not comfortable with the way Johnson's Tonkin Gulf Resolution had been used as a pretext to wage an ever-increasing war. He claimed it "did not give the war powers that the President assumed it gave." He further stated that the SEATO Treaty was misused and that Vietnam was never part of the treaty organization. Member nations of SEATO sent troops as a "mercenary operation paid for by the United States."[73] The question was how to bring Johnson to task for his Vietnam policy and present the position in a cogent, logical, and intellectual manner. Capitalizing on the reform spirit, Laird and Ford devised a series of new groups, or task forces, to handle specific policy areas (domestic and foreign), research them, examine the current policy, and offer some alternatives.

A proposal before the Republican conference advocated a committee concerning planning and research. Charles Goodell was appointed by Ford to chair this group. This committee was designed to give one of Ford's people a top position within the conference leadership. According to Goodell, Ford did not seek permission on this; he just established the committee in order to stave off political problems from conservative Republicans because Goodell was of a more liberal cloth.

The policy committee under Rhodes was separate from planning and research and gave members general direction on votes, guidance on the issues, and so on. It met every week and individual bills coming to the floor were highlighted during the discussion. On the other hand, planning and research developed white papers for specific topics, gathered useful information on other subjects, and helped formulate alternatives for the GOP. As an outgrowth of Goodell's group, task forces were created and included House members as well as researchers. Many of the ideas generated by this effort helped form the Republican platform during the 1968 presidential campaign.

A staff director, Dr. William Prendergast, was appointed for the planning and research committee. He provided form and substance to the new research which numerous members believed was necessary to match the Democrats and their ability to dominate legislative activities. Prendergast had been involved with Republican politics for years and had even made an unsuccessful run for a congressional seat in Maryland. His credentials were impeccable (he had a Ph.D. from the University of Chicago) and research was second nature to him. All of this evolved together and formed a significant move for Republicans who felt out-staffed, out-re-searched, and out-maneuvered in the House. A new era for the minority had arrived.

Planning and research generally met in the Longworth or Cannon Office Buildings; the meetings were irregular, but when they did convene, the committee usually moved to establish a study group or put a research idea into motion, thereby creating the various task forces. Members for planning and research were appointed to this group by their colleagues because they could be trusted to carry out their assignments to the best of their ability. Issues were care-fully chosen in order to keep the party from splitting over liberal-conservative dogma. The composition, then, of this group was that of open-minded people and what Goodell has termed those who sought "aggressive new initiatives."[74]

By 1965 there was a growing recognition within the House lead-ership on the public concern over Vietnam; therefore, two position papers were developed. College students serving as interns were hired with funds from the conference payroll. They were placed under Goodell's charge, while Prendergast coordinated the group. During one summer they were overseen by professors from various universities. All of this had two immediate political benefits: first, it aided Republican congressmen who had taken on these interns; second, these interns did legitimate, valuable work for the confer-ence. Rough drafts of the white papers were given to members of planning and research who sat down and worked out extra details, additions, or deletions. The finished product went to the conference leadership.[75]

Two reports on Vietnam, then, were developed by the Repub-licans in the House; one was published in 1965, the second in 1966. The first goal of each paper was to examine the Vietnam situation from a historical framework and the second purpose was to con-centrate on the administration's role in the entire context of Viet-nam. The final goal was to offer constructive criticism of Johnson's policies.[76] Ford saw the need for research and criticism in the fol-lowing way: "My recollection is that we felt there ought to be an effort made to pull together the history of the Vietnam develop-ments, because I think we foresaw that what was happening was important to the country with some political ramifications."[77] Prendergast has remarked in a similar vein that "Johnson and the Democrats were fond of saying this all began with Eisenhower. They would try and throw it back on a Republican administration. The reports tried to fight this, but the Democrats did not take the alternatives."[78]

Laird felt it was important to make a distinction between Republican and Democratic initiatives on Vietnam. During Eisenhower's term, he faced many familiar choices which would be offered to Kennedy and Johnson. Eisenhower had taken the position that Vietnam was not the place to commit ground troops and this feeling had evolved out of the Korean experience and the 1952 campaign.[79]

Goodell has stated that the only way to unite the party on Vietnam was to take a hawkish stand on the war. The method was to give a particularly negative indictment to Kennedy and a much broader one to Johnson. According to Goodell, they "carefully avoided offering any alternatives." Instead, they offered support for a strong stand, a firm commitment, but not withdrawal. Removal of the American presence was not considered a viable option. A consistent Republican criticism was that American power had to be used in a more effective way. The logic for this, from Goodell's viewpoint, was that Johnson never explained the real commitment; he was not candid about the intelligence reports he received, nor was the President candid with Congress.[80] Consequently, Republicans had to ask the tough questions.

Being candid was a problem in Republican ranks, too, because the GOP was divided on how to criticize LBJ and war policy. Ford felt there should be all out support for the war, especially during 1966. Laird claims the second white paper draft was tough on Johnson, but Les Arends, the House minority whip, and Ford wanted it toned down. Goodell was not in agreement with this, but even Laird has argued that the Republican response did not become more forceful until 1968. In effect, the party was divided and consensus was difficult to achieve. For instance, the 1966 report used the word "miscalculation" in reference to war policy and military direction. This was about as far as the House conference could go in terms of agreement on a key word.[81] Generally, Republicans in the House, except for men like Goodell who never saw Vietnam in the national interest, were hawkish and staunchly anticommunist. For this group, military escalation was necessary to fight communism worldwide, and the final "alternatives" were broad in nature. Members of planning and research saw both white papers before their final draft. They were then forwarded to the conference for discussion and voted on by the entire group.[82]

Not all positions, however, were unanimous. Prendergast has noted the division within Republican ranks and the goals pursued by the House leadership:

The effort of the Republican House leadership was to put aside, soft pedal, differences in points of view among the Republican party. The effort was to present the Republican party as one. In fact, one of the themes that we tried to develop was that the Republican party was—words I remember Laird used once—the only national party, one in which there is real unity about the major public policy issues; whereas the Democrats had a fragmented and divided party.[83]

However, Goodell believes Republicans were uncomfortable with taking responsibility; critiques were easier to give and some congressional leaders resented others on their turf and were reluctant to work with the planning and research group in the House. When Prendergast was asked why he had no counterpart in the Senate, his answer was direct: "I think Dirksen probably considered it an unnecessary appendage. He thought the Senate Policy Committee which did exist, was enough."[84]

Dirksen's entire position on the need for change within the Republican structure seems dubious. For instance, the House white papers were given to Dirksen in his office by Prendergast as part of a "conscious policy," according to Goodell. It was necessary to have Dirksen's approval, a deference which was part of the House leadership's policy. This was done, as Goodell has noted, for a simple reason:

... because Ev Dirksen was trekking up to the White House regularly and dealing with Lyndon Johnson regularly and members of the House leadership were not. We did not want to issue a white paper that Ev Dirksen would attack so we would have him review it. I don't think he made any suggested changes at all, but he knew in advance that we were going to do it. We just didn't want Ev Dirksen asked cold what he thought of this report and say well I haven't even read it, or to make negative comments on it.[85]

Prendergast does not believe Dirksen was sold on Ford's thesis that Republicans needed to develop an overall program. He was satisfied with the status quo. Basically, according to Prendergast, he was "less inclined to rock the boat." He hastened to add, though, that Dirksen was "very skillful" and a "master negotiator" who had a very good relationship with Johnson. When pamphlets or papers were prepared, but not always released, they were shown, as a matter of protocol and necessity, to Dirksen by Prendergast. The two of them would be in Dirksen's office and the motive was to test the senator's reaction. Prendergast has commented, "There was some apprehension that Dirksen might shoot us out of the water once they were released."[86] In other words, he might disavow them. Dirksen, according to Prendergast, insisted on handling the foreign policy issues with the joint leadership while Ford stayed with domestic concerns. Perhaps he was uneasy with what Ford might say about Vietnam, or other areas, or he may have felt his background gave him more expertise.[87] It may even be surmised he wanted to protect his relationship with Johnson by attempting to keep Republican criticism within certain boundaries.

PARTY REVIVAL

Even though significant changes had occurred within the House structure and leadership, and Dirksen continued as a Republican voice in the Senate, the party was faced with a major overhaul. Dean Burch, the national chairman, was replaced by Ray Bliss of Ohio. Bliss's leadership of the Republican National Committee provided some continuity for GOP thought; an outgrowth of this continuity was the creation of the Republican Coordinating Committee.

According to Michigan Governor George Romney, the coordinating committee had its impetus from the Republican Governor's Conference which met shortly after Goldwater's defeat. The governors were concerned about the profound nature of the election results, and it was their wish to organize the GOP in such a fashion so the party would be able to win the presidency in 1968.[88] Mel

Laird also sought this revitalization and was instrumental, along
with Bill Prendergast, in helping organize the coordinating committee. But Ford claimed this new group was the "brainchild of
Ray Bliss," who was the new Republican national chairman.[89]
Whatever the origin, in Laird's judgment its purpose was twofold:
"To bring people together and to have a discussion so that we could
speak more with one voice, and to use our national leadership in
a more effective way."[90] There was a distinct need to overcome
the division caused by the 1964 campaign. Romney, for instance,
accepted Goldwater as a candidate but did not endorse him because
of his civil rights stand and the lack of a position on extremism
within the John Birch Society.[91]

The membership list for the coordinating committee read like a
"Who's Who" of Republican politics. The roster included former
President Eisenhower, all past presidential candidates, a smattering
of governors, and other party officials, but congressional representation was the dominating factor. On January 11, 1965, the congressional joint leadership announced the formation of the coordinating
committee. Dirksen, recognizing the November defeat, emphasized that the GOP would be changing in the future; however, he
reiterated the party's historical role: namely, that the Republican
members of Congress "will guide Republican Party Policy at the
national level, in the absence of a Republican President and Vice
President, by the record they write in the Congress. It is their
responsibility."[92] Gerald Ford, also present at this news conference,
indicated that "the Coordinating Committee will provide a communications center for the exchange of ideas on policy with other
important party leaders and elected officials."[93]

The first meeting of the coordinating committee was held on
March 10, 1965, at the Hotel Willard in Washington. The agenda
spanned a time frame of nearly six hours. Time was alloted for
mini press conferences with reporters in order to publicize the event.[94]
Task forces were formed to cover various national issues; research
was conducted and then a report was made to the overall group.
After discussion of a particular topic, a position paper was issued.
The coordinating committee occasionally would go to Eisenhower's farm at Gettysburg, Pennsylvania. Usually, Eisenhower chaired
the meetings either at his farm or in Washington, and there was a

free flow of ideas even if some members had worked out their
positions ahead of time.[95]

During the opening session in March, the *New York Times* reported that Republicans had already committed themselves to support Johnson's efforts in Vietnam.

In their foreign policy statements, the Republicans said they supported the
Administration's announced policy in defending South Vietnam against
Communist aggression and "deplore the disruptive voices of appeasement
in the Democratic party which undercut the President in his conduct of
foreign affairs at a time of national crisis."[96]

Romney has observed the general feeling among this group was
on the hawkish side even though a few members pushed for a more
moderate stance on behalf of the Republican party. There was a
predominant fear, though, that the men in the field had to be
protected, but by and large most coordinating committee members
supported Johnson.[97]

There was a high degree of cooperation between the House planning and research group and the coordinating committee. Even
though the coordinating committee ran from the Republican National Committee, planning and research helped prepare statements
for the coordinating committee. The coordinating group would
submit statements to planning and research before releasing them
for review by the entire committee. Prendergast is uncertain if this
procedure was paralleled with the Senate Policy Committee, but
he is almost positive a copy went to Dirksen.[98] By June 1965, the
first coordinating committee position paper, or statement, on Vietnam had been completed. The study contained a brief analysis of
why the United States had been fighting in Vietnam and claimed,
essentially, that this struggle was part of a tradition, which had
been supported by Americans for three generations. "In this perspective, the Southeast Asia action is but one example of what we
would recommend as a keystone of contemporary American foreign policy—a firm resistance to communist aggression and communist neo-colonialism wherever it appears."[99]

The policy statement, though, drew a much larger circle because
Vietnam was only one aspect of the Sino-Soviet pressure upon the

world. References were made to Berlin, Korea, and Cuba—each indicative of Marxist pressure. For Republicans, Vietnam was an extension of this process. Direct support for administration policy from the coordinating committee could be found in the following statement:

The Administration's policy in Vietnam today is an attempt to use limited military measures to produce a political result. It is an attempt to set the stage for a diplomatic settlement. The air attacks, and the subsequent intensification of economic and military programs within South Vietnam and Southeast Asia are intended to convince North Vietnam that the United States is determined to use its over-all strength to achieve an end to Communist aggression.

Final recommendations from the coordinating committee to the president were as follows:

1. That the United States specify its purposes in Vietnam as follows:
   a. The elimination of organized violence and political control in South Vietnam by the Viet Cong.
   b. The maintenance of a free and indigenous government of the entire territory of South Vietnam.
   c. Securing border guarantees for Southeast Asia countries.
2. That the United States undertake whatever measures are necessary to attain these objectives including a massive effort to encourage dedication by the people of South Vietnam to achieve their own freedom.
3. That the United States use its influence to call a conference of such nations as will join us in the achievement of the following objectives:
   a. Attainment of military cooperation for the purpose of prosecuting the war.
   b. The economic and social development of South Vietnam.[100]

Ironically, before this report was finished, President Johnson had requested $700 million to finance the American operation in Vietnam. By a House vote of 408 to 7 and 88 to 3 in the Senate, the Congress gave overwhelming support to the administration's request for money within three or four days. According to the *New York Times*,

The display of bipartisanship and unusual speed was designed to show the world that Congress and the country emphatically supported President Johnson's policy of firmness and strength in dealing with communist aggression. Republicans, indeed, were more than happy to support the legislation. As Dirksen said, "I think we have a duty to support the President. . . . He is the Commander-in-Chief."[101]

Key Republican leaders at that time considered the coordinating committee's creation to be a positive step for the party. Richard Nixon, in his memoirs, *RN*, states that Republicans had to close ranks after the 1964 defeat. Neither extreme wing could be allowed to capture the party, and the rank and file had to be convinced that the future was indeed bright. From a point of personal advantage, he knew a healing and rebuilding was in order so the GOP would be unified for a presidential race.[102] Texas Senator John Tower also thought the committee was worthwhile because it helped the GOP capture the White House in 1968. He acknowledged it was not a big win, but in his words, "enough."[103] Ford and Laird also regarded this step as valuable; each agreed there was no way to gain unanimity on everything.

Ford has dubbed the coordinating committee the "guiding hand" for Republicans.[104] Laird even went so far as considering a "shadow cabinet." In this way an advisory group would be developed similar to the English government which gives advice to the prime minister. Through a cabinet-type group, Republicans would have had a spokesman for each area of concern; the coordinating committee could not achieve agreement on specific people to serve this function. There was, according to Laird, a more fundamental political problem because ranking Senate Republicans did not believe their committees should be circumvented. This would have occurred if a person such as Nelson Rockefeller had been brought in to fill one of the advisory positions.[105]

The coordinating committee continued to issue policy statements until the 1968 election. Despite the GOP reorganization and renewal on most levels, the joint leadership still reverted to the traditional mode of responding to Johnson and his Vietnam policy. Dirksen began calling for full unity on Vietnam in early 1965, shortly before and during the opening days of the First Session, Eighty-ninth Congress. As he stated in a *New York Times* interview: "To give up in Vietnam means a loss of force throughout the Orient. The rank of the United States would plummet. And from the standpoint of the Philippines and Guam, we would have no anchor point left."[106] Dirksen may have overstated his case as one looks back, but he saw Vietnam as part of the domino theory vis-à-vis communism. But other members of the party were speaking out as well. Senator Jacob Javits from New York urged LBJ to declare his policy in relation to Vietnam. Speaking at a Lincoln Day Dinner on Long Island, Javits even went as far as supporting the administration's retaliatory air strikes in Vietnam. This support came "within the spirit of bipartisanship."

During a "Meet the Press" interview on January 24, 1965, Dirksen was questioned about Vietnam and the U.S. role therein. He saw three solutions: strike the North, get out, or muddle through in order to stabilize the internal political situation which could eventually provide a military victory. Dirksen emphasized he would not counsel withdrawal due to a geopolitical situation in which the "southernmost flank of the line that runs from Korea to Vietnam and which is our outside defense perimeter [now] will suddenly have that flank turned and then all the trusteed islands in the Pacific as well as the Philippines are in danger and I will not counsel that kind of a course."[107] Although his public stand was usually hawkish, he did, at various times, counsel restraint on the part of Republican leaders. Bill Prendergast has provided a unique perspective to Dirksen's position during 1965 and beyond. According to Prendergast, and through confirmation by another source, Dirksen was more hesitant than most when challenging administration war policy. Prendergast reminisced: "I remember hearing him in meetings, saying 'let's just be quiet, they have the votes.' In fact, he said once, 'When the boxes begin coming back with corpses in them from Vietnam, the American people will react.' "[108]

What is significant, though, is that members of Dirksen's party were reacting, since 1965 was a decisive year for America's commitment to Indochina. By the end of the year, nearly 200,000 troops were in Vietnam and their advisory capacity had given way to a combat role. This shift also was paralleled by increased restiveness among Republican leaders. Nixon, for instance, stated in January, "We are losing the war in Vietnam." He continued, "If our strategy is not changed, we will be thrown out in a matter of months—

certainly within the year."[109] This was part of a new tactic, as one author has written, to be "criticizing the policy-makers."[110] Nixon demanded that air strikes be consistently used to break the supply lines which supported Communist activity in South Vietnam.[111] Goldwater echoed similar sentiments more than a week later for the same treatment. One voice of dissent was New York's John Lindsay, a congressman, who termed Vietnam "the most unwanted war" in American history. He proposed that an international commission be established so that an immediate cease-fire could take place.[112] His call went unheeded.

Eisenhower's position during the first half of 1965 deserves some attention, too. Early on, Johnson saw the value of Eisenhower's public support for his Vietnam strategy. According to Eisenhower biographer Stephen Ambrose, Johnson listened to the ex-president except when it came to the wisdom of actual ground war in Asia. Eisenhower, however, was a hawk and felt Johnson had not done enough to prosecute the war successfully. The reason, according to Ambrose, was that " . . . Eisenhower was far more belligerent, more ready to take extreme action, as an outsider than he had been when he was the man on the spot."[113]

A crucial meeting between Johnson and Eisenhower was held on February 17, 1965, when significant consultation took place between the two. During a meeting which ran close to three hours at the White House, Johnson, along with McNamara, Bundy, and Generals Earle Wheeler and Andrew Goodpaster, listened as Eisenhower explained his views on the American military role in Vietnam and made several key points. First, more support was needed from our NATO allies. Second, the security of Vietnam could not be guaranteed through the use of American troops; rather, the Vietnamese had to stop supplies from reaching the Vietcong. A third area of concern was that morale on our side needed to remain high while we lowered the enemy's. Therefore, cessation and then renewal of air strikes would be ineffective. He argued for continuous pressure and further expansion into North Vietnam's air space. Eisenhower also stated he saw no threat from the Chinese or Soviets. We simply had to pass the word privately that we would take action against them if necessary. Never, he admonished, negotiate from a position of weakness.[114] His final comment, according to Ambrose, was, "We must look at the ef-

fect of our actions on the whole world. When we say we will help
other countries we must then be staunch. It is, of course, necessary to work out tactics, and we should not be unnecessarily
provocative."[115]

Beginning in April 1965, Johnson ordered Goodpaster to serve
as liaison with Eisenhower on a biweekly basis. These meetings
usually went about two or three hours in length and Eisenhower
continued to counsel Johnson to press forward and continue to
fight. According to Ambrose, the former president did warn LBJ
that there was a danger by using draftees in Vietnam because it
might cause a public relations problem.[116]

Eisenhower did begin to express publicly his support during the
spring. Speaking at Grinnell College in Iowa, he said, "None of
us should forget that there is only a single man who can speak for
us on our foreign relations in this critical period. And any inroads
in supporting him would be a disservice to the United States."
Eisenhower agreed many of the things Johnson was now doing had
been recommended the previous year by Goldwater and others.
His response was, "Time changes everything," because, "probably
at that moment it was untimely and shocking to the American
people."[117]

By June 1965, congressional leaders such as Laird were expressing
concern over rumors that the administration might agree to a coalition government in Saigon. Laird saw this as a dangerous shift
in U.S. policy, since more than 50,000 men were serving in Vietnam and believed their lives were "needlessly exposed" if this view
became predominant. Laird expressed the hawkish stand, and, surprisingly enough, Goldwater and Javits embraced a different position. On June 16, 1965, each of these senators gave a speech in
Miami Beach opposing American involvement in an unlimited
ground war. As Goldwater noted:

I do not feel that the expanded use of American ground troops is an effective
addition to the war. The proper ground forces for use in Vietnam are those
of our other allies in the Southeast Asia Treaty Organization. The terrain
and climate are familiar to them and very unfamiliar to us.[118]

Geography aside, the Republican positions were beginning to
vary from time to time. During the latter part of June, Javits won-

dered if we were really welcomed by the Vietnamese and whether regional or United Nations action would be more feasible. On the other hand, only three months earlier Dirksen had reiterated support for a stronger military position. The Senate leader pointed out a paradox: we had supported dictators in Vietnam since the Kennedy administration, but other countries continued to help the North. Those were the same nations with which we were seeking closer ties. Dirksen, however, made Vietnam more than a perimeter of defense. In a television and radio weekly broadcast entitled "A Capsule Story of Vietnam," he briefly outlined the history of Indochina and concluded, "[A]t the moment this show has got to go on unless the world's greatest power is going to have to confess that he was humbled by a little country made up of Communists that we refer to as the Viet Minh under the lead of Ho Chi Minh their Russian trained leader."[119] These sentiments only heightened the pressure upon Johnson in his decisions about Vietnam. One author, quoting from a Gallup Poll taken during the fall of 1965, indicated a surprisingly large portion of the public—64 percent—supported our involvement in Southeast Asia.

The administration, though, may have sensed that all was not well with its Vietnam stance. The continuous barrage from the joint leadership and coordinating committee may have helped persuade Johnson to order a major policy review. On July 21, 1965, the president announced the administration was considering the Vietnam War in light of the economic, military, and foreign policy commitment of the United States. This statement received a lukewarm response on the Republican side, and at a Republican governors' conference in Minneapolis later that month, several demanded that Johnson either take the Vietnam problem to the United Nations or ask Congress for a declaration of war. Romney and fellow Republican Governor Mark Hatfield of Oregon refused to sign a resolution, offered by the governors' conference, which supported the commitment of 155,000 troops for Vietnam. These actions were, for the most part, exceptions to the rule.[120] Rockefeller did not wish to make any political break with the president; rather, he commented that Johnson deserved the "support and backing of all the people."[121]

Two weeks later, at the Herbert Hoover Library in West Branch, Iowa, Richard Nixon delivered an address declaring that we should increase air and sea attacks on North Vietnam. Gerald Ford, a few days later, was urging the White House to "seek more than a settlement with North Vietnam," which for some had the ominous meaning of destroying the Hanoi regime.[122] Whatever the stance, Dirksen took the moderate tone at this juncture by calling for "restraint in any congressional discussion of Vietnam." Earlier in the summer, Mel Laird had urged Johnson to commit himself to a victory over Communist insurgency and drive the Communists out of Vietnam. If he neglected this course, according to Laird, he could be charged with "needlessly exposing" American lives.[123] Laird expressed concern that Johnson might accept a coalition government in Saigon which would force Republicans to withdraw their support of his overseas venture.

All of this dialogue had been prompted by massive raids by B–52s in South Vietnam. Earlier in the year (March, to be precise), Operation Rolling Thunder had begun a sustained bombing of North Vietnam. But Republican strategy was caught in its own cross fire. About one week after Laird's remarks, Dirksen made a general press statement on June 24 that the United States might double its forces to 120,000 men in Vietnam and begin artillery fire into North Vietnam. The article in the *New York Times* said Dirksen "strolled into the Senate press gallery this afternoon to circulate these suggestions without making it clear whether he spoke on behalf of anyone in the Administration."[124] Of course, this tended to weaken the strategy of House Republicans who were seeking clarification for America's role in Southeast Asia.

Nixon, speaking on July 10, said he supported American policy in Vietnam, but he called for critics in the Democratic party to stop undermining Johnson. "The United States today," Nixon said, "is not speaking with one strong voice. The President owes it to the nation to repudiate the critics in his own party."[125] Later in the year he went even further, by advocating a "total embargo" on vessels shipping supplies to North Vietnam so that the war could be brought to a successful conclusion. The idea, of course, was not original, but it did indicate that some Republicans were going to push the issue of Vietnam to further lengths.

The summer of 1965 was a watershed period in terms of U.S. commitment in Southeast Asia. It was a watershed because it was a time when decisions coalesced into a pattern that would continue until 1968, cause dissension within the GOP, and present the world with a degree of American dissension never before witnessed in this century. In their book *The Irony of Vietnam*, Leslie Gelb and Richard Betts have considered whether the Administration policymakers were deceived about events and conditions in Vietnam. Their conclusion rests on the premise that the policymakers deceived themselves by forgetting "qualifying conditions" which were included with various assessments on Vietnam's struggle. Basically, though, incrementalism was the problem. According to Gelb and Betts, "*Incrementalism did not follow from illusion about victory around every corner; it followed from the strategy of progressive pressure and the progressive failure of strategy.*"[126]

Escalation of the war was always regulated by Johnson or Secretary of Defense Robert McNamara, thereby "minimizing autonomy in the field, discouraging the development of comprehensive campaign plans, and refusing to accept bombing proposals in more than weekly target packages. Predictably, this caused intense resentment among the professional soldiers."[127] Johnson also did not really trust the generals, but many in the military never really accepted the peace offensives which were part of the incrementalism. Many feared a repeat performance of Korea—deals or negotiations made at a table while war in the field continued. It seems that Johnson felt trapped between the hawks and doves. No matter which way he moved in the mid–1960s, he faced criticism. Gelb and Betts personify the problem this way: "For one domestic pressure there was a countervailing one; for a J. W. Fulbright there was a John Stennis, for a James Gavin there was a Curtis LeMay, for a Bobby Kennedy and a Eugene McCarthy there was a Barry Goldwater and a George Wallace."[128] Dirksen complicated matters for Johnson, too, by stating, during a "Face the Nation" interview in September, his views on a coalition government in Saigon.

Well, I can only say I hope not. That's a tremendous lure in order to bring hostilities to an end and stop the blood-letting. But will it have been a durable answer if it's done, because if it's neutralist obviously it can go in one direction or another."[129]

In other words, Lyndon Johnson was in the midst of a domestic political quandary and a military quagmire overseas. But there was

more to it than this. Johnson had the military power at his command
to intervene in Vietnam since other areas of the world were relatively quiet. Vietnam was the hot spot and our prestige was on the
line, but it had been placed there by politicians of *both* parties. After
1965 the costs—political, financial, military, and economic—began
to rise. The late 1960s saw Johnson challenged from within his own
party in addition to the loss of crucial Republican support.

By October 1965, organized protests over Vietnam were beginning to surface within the nation. During the weekend of October
16–17, there were draft protests and demonstrations against the
war. These protests so angered Dirksen that he remarked they were
"enough to make any person loyal to this country weep."[130] Although the reaction to these protests was mixed on Capitol Hill, a
turning point in public perception and support of the war had been
reached. The public was beginning to divide on war policy; these
shifting postures would affect the war effort and American politics
on a grand scale. Undoubtedly, the best comment on the Vietnam
War came in late 1965, and it was from Goldwater. On November
2, he called for McNamara's resignation as secretary of defense. He
reminisced that the Democrats had charged that if he were elected,
the war in Indochina would have been intensified and there would
be riots in America's streets. The comment, which was characteristically Goldwater, was, "Well, there has been escalation of the
war in Vietnam and riots in the streets and Goldwater wasn't
elected."[131]

4.

THE OIL CAN AND
THE SWORD

As America entered 1966, several questions plagued war planners: Should we escalate the military commitment? If so, how much? Could a coalition government, including Communist elements, be part of a political structure in Saigon? The previous September, Dirksen had gone on record against a coalition. His statement, coupled with a charge by the coordinating committee that Johnson had been less than candid with the public about war policy and certainly inconsistent with his military options, may have served to put the administration on notice that the political fight was about to intensify. On December 13, 1965, the coordinating committee issued its report on American foreign policy. Sections are worth quoting since the report reflected Republican sentiments; also, within several months the notion of a "credibility gap" would become a catchphrase for the Republican leadership. All of this was addressed by a statement from the coordinating committee:

Questions are being raised both at home and abroad as to the devotion of the American people to peace. One cause of this confusion has been the inability of the Johnson Administration to establish a candid and consistently credible statement of our position in Vietnam. Official statements of the Administration have been conflicting and repeatedly over-optimistic. The Communists have skillfully exploited this inadequacy of our present leadership.

We believe that our national objectives should not be the unconditional surrender of North Vietnam, but unconditional freedom for the people of South Vietnam and support of their struggle against aggression.

Under our present policy in Vietnam, there is a growing danger that the United States is becoming involved in an endless Korean-type jungle war. A land war in Southeast Asia would be to the advantage of the Communists.[1]

In early January, Dirksen, the "hard-line" voice on war policy, publicly broke with LBJ when Dirksen called for a complete victory before engaging in any kind of peace negotiations. Speaking in Washington, he told reporters, "When MacArthur said, 'There is no substitute for victory,' he planted a phrase that is never to be forgotten."[2] Victory for Dirksen was "when the Vietcong lay down their arms." This all may have been in response to Johnson's attempts to negotiate the war behind the scenes. Several days later, Dirksen appeared on ABC's "Issues and Answers" and discussed the peace initiatives. He claimed the president had been informed of the minority position, but reiterated it was their obligation (Republicans as the loyal opposition) to go along with the commander in chief. He added, "[A]nd we have consistently supported him."[3] Also during this interview, Dirksen went so far as to intimate that a blockade, or quarantine, similar to the one used with Cuba might be in order. He further stated his dissatisfaction with the lack of Allied help in Vietnam, but he stopped short of mentioning specific nations.[4]

At this point, it does not appear that Dirksen questioned Johnson's goal of unconditional negotiations at the peace table. But he may have instinctively felt, or feared, this would become strictly an American war. The complete victory would have been the only alternative for Dirksen and the president since withdrawal was tantamount to defeat in the senator's eyes. But the unwillingness to mine North Vietnam's main port, Haiphong, lingered, and the Republicans would continue pressing for such a move.

On January 11, the two congressional leaders were interviewed on NBC's "Today Show." Ford again broached the idea of a quarantine. Dirksen, in a different area, defended his fellow Republicans when questioned about their Senate unity. The minority leader claimed there was bound to be diversity. Ford pointed out there was basic unity in the House but some question on how the United States met its obligation to Vietnam. Dirksen was certain that war would be the dominant issue during 1966; it involved the national security and financial considerations such as taxes or borrowing.

Both leaders agreed that Republicans were going to follow the guidelines set forth by the coordinating committee, but they cautioned the administration about a large-scale ground war in Vietnam. When Dirksen was asked how far Republican support would go, his response was decisive.

Now so long as we have an opportunity to offer our substitutes, our alternatives, our opinions, our suggestions, and they're thrown around the table, and carefully discussed—when the decision is finally made, what to do in the interests of the unity of this country, because you cannot, and you dare not, present a dis-united front to a fevered world, you go along with the Commander-in-Chief.[5]

Ford was equally adamant, but his tone and inferences were different.

Certainly the Republicans ought not to make it a political issue. I think the consequences are too serious, the stakes are too high, as far as the country is concerned. But, if the Commander-in-Chief, or the Administration doesn't run the war well, if they don't do things that protect our best interests in the minds of the American people, the people themselves will make the issue.[6]

Within several days of Dirksen's intonations, Lyndon Johnson delivered the annual State of the Union Address before Congress. During the speech he discussed Vietnam in some detail, and in one part said:

Tonite the cup of peril is full in Vietnam. That conflict is not an isolated episode, but another great event in the policy that we have followed with strong consistency since World War II. . . .

We seek neither territory nor bases, economic domination or military alliance in Vietnam. We fight for the principle of self-determination that the people of South Vietnam should be able to choose their own course, choose it in free elections without violence, without terror, and without fear.[7]

In order to counter Johnson's delivery and free air time, Republicans adopted a new approach. The House conference developed a unique concept called the Minority State of the Union Address. The networks were reluctant to give the GOP coverage because the audience was not thought large enough and there would be a sacrifice in terms of revenue.[8] Today, of course, the opposition's rebuttal is an accepted practice, but at this juncture the GOP was charting new ground.

On January 17, Republicans delivered their "State of the Union Address" in reply to the administration. Dirksen and Ford gave a televised speech before nearly one hundred members of Congress in the old Supreme Court Chamber of the Capitol. In what was to become a familiar pattern, Ford concentrated on domestic issues while Dirksen took foreign affairs. The senator from Illinois described Vietnam as "a grim, bloody and costly business . . . which was . . . not of our making." He reiterated a traditional GOP theme: "to retreat and get out would be deemed a confession that we are a paper tiger, and . . . to forsake our pledges would shatter confidence in us and further diminish our prestige." Even though he endorsed administration policy, he drew no applause from the Republicans present, whereas Ford was interrupted by applause sixteen times as he attacked domestic programs. However, in the same breath, Dirksen seemed to offer the olive branch to LBJ when he advocated the following course:

Let the peace efforts continue. Who can object to any honorable effort to secure peace when young blood is involved? Let the military effort continue. It demonstrates our determination to keep our word. Let it be intensified if necessary as sound military judgment dictates. There is, after all, no substitute for victory.[9]

The senator, therefore, wanted the best of both worlds. His statements indicate if the pressure was continuously applied, then results were sure to follow. If sound military judgment sought escalation, so be it. The key maxim to remember, though, was that Dirksen had no *direct* control over war policy; it was in the hands of Johnson.

The aforementioned vignette also illustrates the basic differences between the two Republican leaders. Ford has noted that a newsman coined the phrase "that Everett Dirksen was the oil can and I was the sword." Ford also has commented, "Everett always had a tendency to be less strident than I, but it never interfered with our personal relationship or overall Republican strategy."[10]

Despite all the speeches, statements, interviews, personal conferences, and GOP strategy, it appears they had little collective impact upon the commander in chief. Johnson, though, was still grateful for Dirksen's support. Through presidential Press Secretary Bill Moyers, he said, "Mr. Dirksen's statement was consistent with the tradition of a 'Loyal Opposition.' "[11] In accordance with this bipartisan spirit, a meeting was held at the White House on January 25, 1966, for a Vietnam briefing. At this conference, Johnson indicated there might be a cessation of the current bombing pause and an escalation in the fighting.

During the early part of 1966, Republican leaders outside Congress were expressing concern over direction of the war. Romney went so far as to suggest a congressional debate and possible declaration of war if American military support increased and our forces were no longer confined to a defensive posture.[12]

Nixon, supporting Johnson's bombing halt for the purpose of increasing the peace initiative, did not believe foreign nations should receive American aid if they traded with North Vietnam. It was noted also that if war continued in Asia until the fall, the Democrats would have a "liability" according to Nixon.[13] Questioned in late January on ABC's "Issues and Answers," the former vice president responded to the statement that Republican support for Johnson had made the war a political cause. He responded, "I hope it will not be an issue. It will become one only if President Johnson fails to take a strong line that will preserve the peace by refusing to reward the aggressors." Nixon further stated that Democrats who had "taken the soft line, the appeasement line," would be subject to Republican criticism.[14]

Johnson did not resume the bombing of North Vietnam in early February. Eisenhower offered his public support and cautioned LBJ about the approach to privileged sanctuaries. Romney, speaking in New Hampshire during mid-February, noted the approach but also commented that Congress had not really been consulted. Consequently, the commitment overseas "does not have the degree of public understanding" which was necessary for success.[15]

Johnson, assailed from within by his own party, was buoyed by the moves of the forty-one governors in mid-November when they adopted a resolution supporting administration efforts in Vietnam. The resolution offered by Republican Governor James Rhodes of Ohio was seconded by Rockefeller. This action came after a three-

hour briefing at the White House by the president and other administration officials. Romney did not attend the governors' meeting,
but Republican Governor John Reed of Maine remarked that Vietnam never should have been a political issue. He observed that
Republican support in the Congress had been stronger than the
Democratic support. Rockefeller, on a more philosophical note,
remarked that it was not the time for politics. Rather, "It is a time
for study and analysis and deep concern for those who have given
their lives and are risking their lives."[16]

Rockefeller's comment is interesting from the standpoint that
Congress was beginning to examine the American role in South
Vietnam. Vice President Hubert Humphrey returned from a nine-
nation tour of Asia and briefed congressional leaders on his obser-
vations during a meeting at the White House. Republican congres-
sional leaders gave him high praise. Humphrey also journeyed to
Capitol Hill and testified before an Executive Session of the Senate
Foreign Relations Committee on March 2.

Division and discord were the rule of the day within the Democratic party. As we noted earlier, the personification of this dissent
was J. William Fulbright. He not only chaired the Foreign Relations
Committee but also was one of the most outspoken critics concerning the American role in Vietnam. Of course, Fulbright had
helped push the Gulf of Tonkin Resolution in August 1964 but
later broke with the administration. He reminisced many years later
about Lyndon Johnson and his lack of expertise with foreign policy:
"President Johnson was a fine man in many respects. He was a
powerful individual, but he had no experience whatever, and very
limited education, in anything other than domestic politics. He just
made a serious mistake in judgment."[17] Fulbright continually re-
minded Johnson about his errors. But Humphrey's testimony before the Foreign Relations Committee was received by at least one
Republican senator as a "pep talk" which was designed to get people
out "and preach the gospel" about Vietnam.[18] Despite Humphrey's
cheerleader approach, the cleavage in Democratic ranks was on the
rise.

Republicans took note of this breach when the House Republican
Policy Committee pointedly declared that the nation and the world
were waiting for Johnson to take command of his party by issuing
a written statement that "the deep division within the Democratic

Party over American policy in Vietnam is prolonging the war, undermining the morale of our fighting men and encouraging the Communist aggressor."[19] Gerald Ford even went so far as to pledge that Republicans would not make Vietnam an election issue in the fall of 1966. If it became an issue, according to Ford, then Americans would make it one since the Democrats were so split. Nixon, in his characteristic forcefulness, went even further when he claimed that should America adopt the stance of J. William Fulbright, which was "the appeasement line, . . . we will be in World War III within four to five years." If the United States, according to Nixon, "cuts and runs in Vietnam we will have a temporary peace and then a certain world war."[20]

The political irony here, of course, was that Republicans, and Dirksen in particular, were most supportive of Johnson. In a television and radio weekly broadcast during late February 1966 entitled "The Commander and Chief," Dirksen gave a mini civics lesson on the war powers of Congress and the military control which belonged to the president. Dirksen drew the analogy with the Civil War and said that many had tried to tell Lincoln how to direct war policy, but ultimately the decision was the president's. He chose to make a further parallel by comparing critics of that time with critics of the current period. The point was obvious: criticism of the war was unjustified since the president had power over it. The civics lesson went on to discuss the prerogatives of power.

Now out in Vietnam you get problems like this. Shall we bomb Hanoi or not bomb Hanoi, or shall we plant mines in all those water courses and water fingers that stretch out from Haiphong Harbor and it is really a tremendous layout there and there are so many approaches before you get up to Haiphong. Well you know you have mine layers and when a vessel comes in touch with one of these submerged mines, it explodes and the chances are that they'll rip such a hole in the vessel that in the absence of any immediate rescue it'll probably sink. So that's a tremendous responsibility but somebody has to make the decision.

Now then there is the question of escalation of the war . . . that again is ultimately a decision that the President as Commander in Chief of the Armed Forces must make.

Then of course there's the question of withdrawal. There are some people who think we should withdraw from Vietnam. Well, who shall make the decision? Who shall finally tell our Joint Chiefs of Staff and our field generals that we'll get out, we'll bring the troops and whatever weapons we have left back home? That's a decision that finally must be made by the Commander in Chief.[21]

What all of this indicates, essentially, is that Dirksen was placing the responsibility for war policy on Johnson's shoulders. Constitutionally, this is where it belonged; politically, it helped absolve Dirksen, at least, from direct connection with the war. He could offer alternatives, but Johnson made the final decision. All of this would sustain the senator and the Republicans if the war went sour, which it would certainly do in the near future. Consequently, there was a feeling that this was Johnson's war. Representative John Rhodes, chairman of the House Policy Committee, was quoted as saying, "We don't want to tell the President how to run his war," but he did not want it referred to as "Johnson's war," which, therefore, coined a new phrase within the American political scene.[22]

Concerns also were expressed in this vein by Congressman Bob Wilson of the Republican House Campaign Committee. Wilson, who had served on the House Armed Services Committee for many years, thought Johnson was devious with troop planning and movements. According to Wilson, it was difficult to know the precise strategy or military movement because the administration kept a fairly tight lid on this sort of information.[23] Publicly, Laird echoed the same feeling in late April. He blamed Johnson for a failure to be frank and honest with the people about the objectives and progress of the war in Southeast Asia.[24]

During March 1966, the joint leadership gave two press conferences. Dirksen scored the administration for failing to reassure the people and Congress about domestic matters (inflation and taxes); he also was critical because "the war in Vietnam is escalating but the Administration has not informed the American people how big it will get nor how costly it will become." Ford, on the other hand, complained that Johnson's "credibility gap" had grown to a "credibility canyon." The notion of a credibility gap had already surfaced in Washington anyway and was being used by some in the press corps who doubted the validity and frankness of administration responses to their questions. They believed that Johnson's policy on Vietnam was dividing his own party more than the Republicans.[25]

Gerald Ford, like Everett Dirksen, presented somewhat of a paradox. Ford admits that his canyon statement was a combination of actual feeling and political rhetoric. His relationship with Johnson was cordial and he felt the president listened to his proposals and suggestions. However, Ford also had a responsibility to publicly criticize Johnson. It was a political duty and one which he accepted.[26] On April 18, 1966, in a speech at Tonawanda, New York, Ford charged that the administration had made "tragic mistakes" in its Vietnam policy and said it was an example of "shocking mismanagement." He claimed LBJ was to blame for the political dissension in Vietnam which had been caused, according to Ford, by the president showing too much attention to certain political figures in Saigon. The week prior to his New York speech, the House minority leader charged that the administration had allowed a bomb shortage (750 pound size) to exist and that delays in Vietnamese harbors impeded the movement of supplies to our troops and the war effort.[27] This entire set of statements precipitated a bombing run of its own; this time with Republicans. Instead of aiming the shots at Johnson, Republicans began to fire at themselves.

The following day, Dirksen openly disassociated himself from Ford's statement. Speaking from the Senate press gallery, Dirksen could not agree with the term "shocking mismanagement" and said, "I just don't deliver hard judgments like that unless I have some hard facts." He insisted, however, his statements were not intended as a criticism of Ford. But according to the *New York Times*, some reporters present saw an indirect criticism of the House minority leader when Dirksen added, "You don't demean the chief magistrate of your country at a time like this, so far as the war is concerned."[28] Finally, Dirksen was asked if the party should be speaking with a more unified voice, especially after Laird and Ford had criticized the Democrats for division on Asian policy. His reply was that "in a free land there will always be some dissidence," and he further stated that Republicans "get as much consensus as we can get."[29]

The next day Dirksen denied that he and Ford had split over war policy and declared, "I'm the most misunderstood man in the world."[30] He claimed reporters had misinterpreted what had been said the previous day. Dirksen acknowledged that Ford had followed the shortage idea more closely but emphasized that he needed more information before taking such a stand.

Obviously, the break had taken place and the GOP tried to heal the wound, so, on April 21, Ford admitted he had unconfirmed information on the management of the war. He made this statement with Dirksen present and it appears that all this was done to squelch rumors of a major split between the leadership.[31] Years later, Ford claimed there was no significant disagreement with Dirksen over the areas already outlined and said this "never ruptured our basic cooperation." Ford had his sources—committee contacts and in the Pentagon—but declined to name them specifically. Instead, he chose to characterize them as "credible" and "valid."[32]

The team of Gerald Ford and Everett Dirksen represented an unusual mix on Capitol Hill. Ford had great respect for the elder Dirksen and has noted an acceptance by the senator even though they were of a different background and age group. According to Ford, "I admired him for his intellect, his astuteness, his communications capability, and I liked him as a person." Ford typecast Dirksen as a shrewd individual who had a "great knack of understanding the political path that was desirable from his point of view and the point of view of the party, and I think the country too."[33]

Bill Prendergast, another observer on the scene, has noted that several months later the joint leadership went to individual questions of the week. According to Prendergast, "Dirksen, because of his personality, and flamboyant style, tended to dominate these events."[34] Of course, the joint leadership would have press conferences in the future, and they normally would be arranged in advance. A question of the week would be considered, and material developed to back up that issue since a discussion would take place during the news conference. Ford has confirmed the question was agreed to in advance so there would be continuity with their attack.[35] This strategy also allowed for some Republican consistency when they were meeting reporters and questioning Johnson's policies. It also helped defuse potential problems such as those from April 1966.

The spring of 1966 witnessed domestic turmoil in Saigon, and

American field casualties were about twice as high as the Vietnamese. By late May, Dirksen was advocating a briefing for congressional leaders on the war. From his vantage point the time had arrived for a "thorough discussion of the diplomatic, military, and political situation in Vietnam."[36] The request for a meeting was renewed through a joint leadership press conference. At this juncture, Dirksen openly declared that the president was neither "candid" nor "consistently credible" about his policies vis à vis Vietnam. He asked the question: "Mr. President, What *CAN* we believe?"[37] All of this, of course, had a strange ring, especially after the senator had chastized Ford for his remarks, but in June they fit his purpose which was seemingly to force Johnson into a White House meeting about the war.

The administration vigorously denied charges from the joint leadership, but it did not outwardly accept or reject Dirksen's proposal. Presidential Press Secretary Bill Moyers did, however, indicate that Everett Dirksen was welcome at the White House any time and could bring any senator of his choice. Dirksen took Johnson up on the offer and met with the president but still wanted a bipartisan meeting. The White House finally agreed and the meeting was held on June 11. The briefing included six Democrats and seven Republican congressional leaders; among the topics covered was Vietnam. Dirksen emerged from the meeting and said that the Vietnam situation had been given "a slightly hopeful cast," but he did not elaborate.[38]

Other Republicans, such as Ford, must not have shared the Illinois senator's enthusiasm. Speaking at commencement exercises at Parsons College in Iowa, Gerald Ford claimed the administration was not doing enough to hold down casualties, nor were they attempting to end the war. He predicted "that we are approaching a large-scale land war in Asia."[39] Several days later, during an interview on ABC's "Issues and Answers," the House minority leader declared, "The American people will not stand for a long-drawn-out large-scale military conflict." Ford also urged Johnson to expand the attacks on North Vietnam; otherwise Republicans would be forced to fight the president on his failure to pursue the war fully. He further speculated that by November the voters might register their dissent at the polls if Johnson did not use the power at his command.[40] Nine days later, the president did expand the war by ordering American bombers to attack oil installations at Haiphong and Hanoi.

Some Republicans, though, were not happy with this action. Senator Jacob Javits called it a "risky" and "chancy" move while Senator George Aiken declared, "Instead of lessening the war it will expand it and it won't shorten it." Ford, on the other hand, said the entire strike should have taken place "months ago."[41] Similar sentiments were echoed by other Republican leaders. Romney argued that we could not "bring the North Vietnamese to the bargaining table by simply saying that you are going to demonstrate to them that they can't win."[42] Bombing, then, was an acceptable course to pursue, but Romney still opposed a "blank check" endorsement of Johnson's Vietnam policy.[43]

Nixon had gone to Vietnam to gather military and political information during the summer of 1966. He hastened to add he did not intend to use it against Democrats in the congressional campaign later that year. While on tour in South Vietnam, he denounced Johnson's critics and claimed this form of dissent only prolonged the conflict and prevented negotiations from being realized. He noted, "Nothing will help more to win this war than to have a unity of purpose." He also speculated that "Possibly the election can achieve this." Again, Nixon observed the American goals in Vietnam were not properly articulated.[44] Upon further reflection a few days later, Nixon argued that American unification was needed in the struggle to combat communism in Asia. "Further debate," according to the Republican leader, "can only delay the end of the war." The excessive criticism of Johnson only served to "encourage the enemy."[45]

By the summer of 1966, divisions were apparent in Republican ranks over the use of conventional air power. In an ironic twist, however, the GOP became a source of support, and maybe even strength, for Lyndon Johnson. For most Republicans, bombing or some sort of negotiations were the only significant alternatives. Author Eric Goldman, who was a presidential assistant during LBJ's administration, has asserted that the president shifted towards conservatives and their views because he found them to be more understanding and supportive. As time passed, and public pressure increased, Goldman saw Johnson even go to the extreme of having members of the Presidential Scholars program cleared by the FBI before they were selected to work with his administration. The motive was to keep dissenters, or those connected with peace activists, away from the White House and the president.[46]

The nation's restiveness with the Vietnam War became apparent as the war continued and casualties increased. During June 1966, Nixon gave the commencement address at the University of Rochester in New York. As part of his speech, he discussed the concept of academic freedom and noted the increased hostility towards the war on college campuses. His remarks were particularly poignant since they reflected the growing disenchantment and realization that America was being polarized by an overseas war. For Nixon, the abuse of academic freedom had occurred when "any teacher who uses the forum of a university to proclaim that he welcomes victory for the enemy in a shooting war crosses the line between liberty and license. If we are to defend academic freedom from encroachment, we must also defend it from its own excesses." Nixon carefully affirmed the principle that this freedom included "to be against war, to be against this war, to be against the way this war is conducted, to be against the inequities of the draft." He also reiterated his belief that the current conflict had to be waged to prevent World War III.[47]

Throughout the summer, the House Republican Conference had been overseeing a white paper which was being prepared by the committee on planning and research. The document would be issued in late September, but another maneuver was occurring and its genesis came from within the party. A new policy concerning Vietnam was formed, the essence of which was an all-Asian concept of negotiating an end to the war. Richard Nixon had announced this proposal and he was receiving solid support from politicians like Ford, Tower of Texas, Case of New Jersey, and Eisenhower. The gist of Nixon's proposal rested on the premise that America was a Pacific power, but not an Asian power; therefore, the problem of Vietnam needed to be settled by Asian nations with American help and influence.[48] Interviewed on the "Today Show;" Nixon maintained, "We need new tactics, new leadership, new methods to shorten this war and bring it to a conclusion without appeasement of the enemy."[49] Even though this idea received backing by the joint leadership, Dirksen remarked, "We would not necessarily be bound by its conclusions." When pressed further, the senator argued that if the Asian proposal did not work out in our favor then we would not be bound by its proposals.[50]

By late September, Johnson agreed to attend a conference in Manila to discuss the Asian situation. Those nations sending representatives were South Vietnam, the Philippines, South Korea, Thailand, Australia, and New Zealand. Although Ford felt LBJ might have sought the trip "as an alternative to campaigning at home," he and Dirksen endorsed the meeting as a positive step, especially since Republicans had urged such a move.[51] Even the coordinating committee issued a statement extending good wishes to Johnson on his Manila visit, but they also noted the event could have been held six months earlier, or even a year before. The committee statement stressed the quest for peace, but further elaborated with the hope "that the conference will produce a significant increase in military, economic, and politicial support from our allies."[52] The predominant feeling was that an extra effort from allied troops could relieve our military burden in the field.

As the fall campaign began, Nixon took to the stump on behalf of Republican candidates. Speaking before the annual American Legion Convention in Washington on August 31, he claimed there was a tendency for the loyal opposition to criticize everything. In his judgment, this was a mistake when the criticism concerned Vietnam, since men were fighting and dying there. He urged unity to be forthcoming from the president on down and offered a dire prediction that "if Vietnam falls, the Pacific will be transformed into a Red ocean and the road will be open to a third world war."[53] During September, in a Utah speech, he stressed the need to reduce ways in which war supplies entered North Vietnam (i.e., bombing their ports), and he also suggested to the audience that electing a substantial number of Republicans in November would "give strength to the loyal opposition" thereby allowing the GOP a more sound consensus on the war.[54] Nixon was concerned that divided Democrats were the chief obstacle to peace. On several other occasions he warned against large troop increases overseas because even if we won the war, "we would have on our hands a dependency for a generation to come."[55] He also predicted Johnson would increase troop levels after the election because the administration was trying to create the impression that its Vietnam policy needed no revision. Instead of increasing the manpower, Nixon offered an easier solution: quarantine North Vietnam and increase aerial bombardment.[56]

Even though Nixon was strident with his remarks, the opening salvo for the GOP in the fall election was the release of a second white paper prepared by the committee on planning and research under Goodell. Although it was a re-working of the other document from 1965, it came at an opportune time—shortly before the mid-term elections. During a joint leadership meeting, Ford called Dirksen's attention to the document and requested he review it in the event that questions came from reporters at the press conference the next day.[57] In this second paper, Johnson bore the brunt of criticism.

The Administration has not told the American people the truth about the military situation in Vietnam, about the mission of American troops, about war costs, about casualties, about peace feelers. This studied deception strikes at the vitals of the system of popular government.[58]

The report again traced U.S. involvement with Indochina from Truman to Kennedy. It further argued our war strategy was incorrect, the administration policy inconsistent, and it asserted the administration lacked candor in dealing with the nation. In a closing, almost prophetic, remark, the report concluded with the following statements:

Administration policy has prevented Communist conquest of South Vietnam. However, peace or victory or stability there are still remote. Faced with a prospect of war for five to seven years, of the spread of conflict to Thailand and perhaps other parts of Southeast Asia, of Communist China equipped with nuclear weapons, the United States must give attention to basic questions about its future political and military strategy in Asia.

A five-year war in Vietnam would, at the present rate, involve the frightful cost of 125,000 American casualties. This high cost is dwarfed by the catastrophic losses which South Vietnam would suffer in five more years of fighting. To the South Vietnamese and other threatened people of Asia, this type of limitless war may come to be an unattractive alternative to Communist domination.

The urgent immediate question facing the nation is how to end this war more speedily and at smaller cost while safeguarding the independence and freedom of South Vietnam.[59]

The supposition of this report rested on the hope that Americans were seeking new leadership and direction, especially in war policy. The document helped serve as a statement by the loyal opposition to demonstrate weaknesses in the president's actions. This second report was more harsh on Johnson and seemed less insistent on bipartisan support for the commander in chief.

As the election drew near, the political rhetoric grew in ferocity. On October 13, 1966, Dirksen expressed concern, during a joint leadership press conference, that Johnson was still not telling the truth about Vietnam.

We are concerned that an all-Asian Peace Conference—a practical first step toward peace in Vietnam—has now been summarily rejected as a peace hope. We are concerned—for we are convinced—that the American people are not being told the whole truth about their Government and the Administration's plans for them.[60]

Johnson had charged that Republicans "were afraid of their own shadows," offered "no constructive programs," and "didn't know how to end the war in Vietnam." The following day Dirksen responded to the president's charges. "Is the President bewildered? Was he referring to his own Administration? His statements actually spell out the most damning political self-indictment in modern political history."[61]

Nixon, never one to be left out of a partisan battle, assailed Johnson for his irresponsible charges against the loyal opposition. For Nixon, the situation was pristine.

Republicans have stood behind the President in his efforts to deny reward to aggression. Republicans have refused to undercut the United States position in Asia for partisan gains.

It has been the President's party that has harbored those who have counseled appeasement of Communist aggression in Vietnam.

It has been the 25 Democratic senators and 90 Democratic congressmen whose cries for peace at any price has given heart to Hanoi—and thus been directly responsible for encouraging the enemy, prolonging the war and lengthening the risk of American casualties.[62]

Nixon went on to draw a parallel between the 1966 election and the position that Woodrow Wilson was in during 1918 and 1919. Wilson had attempted to retain a Democratic majority in Congress during the midterm elections of 1918 and failed. By the time he sailed for the Versailles Peace Conference in 1919, his political support in Congress had dwindled. What Johnson needed was support, and, like Wilson, he would not receive it; this would all come to bear in 1968. Essentially, Johnson would have a control by the majority party in Congress; they were, however, divided on policy just as Americans were in 1919.

Here again, during the fall campaign of 1966, the consistent themes were reiterated: lack of candor, misuse of military power, and missed attempts at peace. If the lack of candor and truth was a rallying point for Republicans, their role required more than incessant criticism in this area. Nixon, seizing the opportunity and initiative, proposed in late October and early November a bipartisan approach to ending the war victoriously. He noted that if fighting was not concluded by 1968, it would become a "devastating political issue."[63] Even though Nixon had consistently supported the war aims, he advocated the traditional GOP position of increased military power to win. He also suggested an economic offensive, elements of which had been proposed by others. His concise proposal contained the following points:

No American aid of any kind be sent to any nation that trades with or aids the Communist enemy in North Vietnam.

No loans or grants be extended by the United States to the Communist countries of Eastern Europe which continue to trade with Hanoi and Havana. Nor should the American Government guarantee commercial credits to such countries or to the Soviet Union.

No export licenses be issued for any strategic materials to be sent to the Soviet Union while Soviet advisors and Soviet missiles are engaged in the business of killing American pilots in Vietnam.

Foreign trading companies that choose to profit from trading with Havana and Hanoi be denied the right to profit from trading with the United States. American ports should be closed to the ships of any such trading company.[64]

Clearly, Nixon had set the tone for the Republican party during the midterm campaign and he emerged as one of the top spokesmen concerning American policy in Vietnam. His speeches helped formulate his thoughts as he considered a run for the White House in 1968. Dirksen and Ford used their leadership positions to offer formulas, suggestions, and criticisms on war policy. Republicans in general concurred with the overall administration goals for Vietnam: a nation not hampered by fifth column or terrorist activities and a nation seeking to be free. But there was still a need for advocating alternatives to Johnson's use of military power, and the irony, which Nixon noted at this time, was that there would be a half-million men in Vietnam the following year if Lyndon Johnson fought the kind of war that the Communists wanted. Essentially, Nixon had posed three questions during the campaign: (1) what kind of war was being waged—full-scale or limited?; (2) how would manpower requirements be determined with the use of extra air and sea support?; and (3) how would the war be financed in view of the large domestic expenditures?

All of the key Republican leaders were caught in a delicate situation. Loyalty to the country, loyalty to the party, and, above all, protecting our men in the field were positions that had to be considered. To criticize constructively required a careful analysis, and alternatives were slim because they agreed with Johnson in principle. One observer who saw this first hand was William Baroody, Jr., who served as a top aide to Mel Laird. Baroody has commented that the Republican leadership, in the House especially, *agonized* over their proper role as the loyal opposition.

According to Baroody, congressional leaders "took very seriously their role as leaders in a political process and with respect to the impact they would have on their country and their country's policies." They struggled with the options of working privately behind the scenes to affect policy changes or going public and, "building the consensus and fire behind a change in policy." Guidelines and precedents were difficult to find and the leadership struggled over the correct path because of moral, patriotic, and political considerations. Baroody has also noted, "You're not going to pick up a civics book and come up with a formula that applies to all situations."[65]

Despite all the political rhetoric and effort, the voters rejected the Republican attempt to become the majority on Capitol Hill. Their net gain was forty-seven seats in the House and three in the Senate. By regaining some of the lost ground from two years earlier, some of the reorganization was beginning to pay dividends. The coordinating committee and joint leadership cannot be evaluated only on the basis of promoting campaign issues. Each group provided a political forum, but the coordinating committee served a distinctive purpose, as did planning and research, since they allowed the various Republican factions and elements to interact, thereby developing stronger personal and party ties. By refraining from haggling, which had plagued it in the past, the GOP was able to present a more unified front as it worked towards a crucial political victory in 1968. Bill Baroody captured the spirit of this new momentum when he said, "The party was then in transition and going from simply the party of opposition to the party of constructive Republican alternative proposals."[66]

Vietnam, as a crucial political topic, would not recede into the background. America's military role expanded with LBJ's practice of incrementation. All of these conditions set the stage for the next two years when the war became the dominant issue within our society.

THE YEAR OF DEMARCATION: 1967

Two opposing political forces were at work during the early stages of 1967; a president of the United States sought to reinforce his slipping position, and Republicans hoped to chip away at his existing position. Lyndon Johnson, during this year, would begin to lose his grip on the political structure and the Republican party was more than willing to help him along.

During January, Johnson delivered his State of the Union Address before a Joint Session of Congress and a nationwide television audience. This was the kind of forum that Johnson relished since he could state his case directly to the people. Republican congressional leaders continued their policy of responding to Johnson, and, on January 19, Ford and Dirksen presented their case against LBJ. As in the past, Ford concentrated on domestic concerns while Dirksen reviewed the foreign policy situation.

When Johnson addressed the nation and the Congress, he noted the high cost of Vietnam. Dirksen agreed with the president's forth-right statements that our costs in lives and agony would be high. Dirksen further stated:

Let us make plain to the world that we mean business! We are in this war to carry out our commitments. To do less would be to break our pledge. In this grim undertaking, a teaspoonful of gospel is not enough. We must do all that is necessary until the freedom and independence of Vietnam are assured.

He also reiterated that Republicans stood as the loyal opposition with emphasis on loyalty. The senator then posed a pointed question: If we were to negotiate a peace over Vietnam, with whom would we negotiate, and what would be our stance at the peace table? Publicly, Dirksen asked the administration, "What policy will we be asked to support?"[67]

Everett Dirksen also was expanding his concern over public disorder during 1967. Late in October 1966, in his annual report, he quoted from Franklin Roosevelt, "The Government's house is not in order." In his report for the Eighty-ninth Congress, second session, he cited Vietnam as the longest and third largest war in American history. He charged that American prestige abroad had fallen to a new low despite the $120 billion spent in foreign aid. Dirksen further stated that republicans in the Senate had given the President full support when he sought extra appropriations for defense, plus an additional authorization of $415 million in aid to Vietnam.[68] By beginning his tough stance in late 1966, and continuing it in early 1967, it is evident that he wanted to separate himself from the administration. However, he still used the carrot-and-stick approach with Johnson. On one hand, he delivered tirades against fiscal mismanagement, war tactics, and so on; then he evoked a sense of pride by commenting on Republican support. In effect, he gave the impression that the GOP formed a solid wall of support, or resistance when necessary. This, of course, was not the case, and one can only speculate whether Johnson saw through the charade. During a news conference on February 2, 1967, the president responded to all of his critics, especially the political voices:

I'm going to do with the Congress like I'm trying to do with our adversaries in other places in the world—I'm going to say to the minority party, who

I do think appears to be able to find fault with almost every act, that I want to meet them halfway and I want their cooperation. I want their help because I don't believe that it's good for the country to have partisan political infighting all the time.[69]

The Congress did not remain silent either. Democrats became increasingly restive as the costs of war escalated. New York's Senator Robert F. Kennedy had proposed a suspension of the bombing over North Vietnam to induce the Communists to the peace table. Dirksen disagreed with his Senate colleague and stood steadfastly behind the administration when it refused a cessation of bombing without equivalent action by the other side. By late March, Dirksen was still espousing the hawkish view. After a White House meeting, he predicted that bombing attacks would intensify.

When you are at war and the enemy refuses to talk except on terms that would mean your surrender, you turn the screws on him. You cut off his supply lines and his source of food and do everything necessary to bring him down.[70]

Charles Percy, junior senator from Illinois and Dirksen's Republican colleague, stated earlier in March "that the enemy [should] show some evidence of good faith before unilateral cessation of the bombing."[71] About three weeks later, Republican Senator Edward Brooke from Massachusetts, and a newly elected member of the Ninetieth Congress, came out in favor of the war after completing a two-week tour of Southeast Asia when he remarked, "If we show strength, I believe he [Ho Chi Minh] will come to the peace table sooner."[72]

Even though Johnson had been receiving a lot of support from GOP senators, George Romney began to publicly chide the president on war policy and even went so far as to offer a "new" Republican position. In mid-February, Romney called for new directions in American foreign policy by asserting that containment used by Truman and Eisenhower was no longer effective. His critique reflected the political oratory of the time when he said, "The facts are that the Johnson Administration, despite its vast power and lofty rhetoric is old and tired. Its leadership has failed and must be replaced." There was, according to this Republican, a need for "primary emphasis on brotherhood rather than primarily on guns, gadgets, and things for being the world's policeman."[73] Romney saw the pacification program in rural South Vietnam as a failure because Communist aggression existed and the indigenous population was in revolt.[74] However, when he charged Johnson with "political expediency" on conduct of the war, he refused to detail his charge when pressed by reporters.[75]

These attacks upon the president's policies grabbed media attention since Romney was a potential presidential candidate for 1968, and eventually he had to delineate his views on the war. He finally gave the long-awaited summary during early April. Basically, George Romney did not advocate withdrawal from Vietnam but urged that negotiations for ending the war continue. He argued that critics only oversimplified the alternatives in Vietnam if they concentrated on bombing and withdrawal. He did, however, urge that necessary force be used to protect our men in the field and stop supplies and troops infiltrating from North Vietnam. Romney recognized South Vietnam's struggle had to be won by combating guerrilla warfare in conjunction with political and psychological warfare since the Vietcong were more nationalistic than Communist. Above all, he did not want the United States to enter the internal struggle since the military role had already been Americanized. The final statement of Romney's detailed Vietnam position was typically Republican and probably designed to deflect charges that he was soft in his stand. He said, "For what it is worth, I would like to tell them right now that here is one Republican I can speak for who will not settle on their terms under any circumstances."[76]

By spring, Republicans, guided by personal and political convictions, were beginning to face a split within their ranks. It must be remembered that the diversity existed from the potential presidential contenders, senators, congressmen, and party leaders; they were staking out their turf and watching the public mood very carefully. The Senate did pass a resolution supporting Johnson in a limited war—not an expanded one—during early March. This was the first formal resolution since the Gulf of Tonkin and the vote was 72 to 19.[77] Several weeks later, though, the nation's governors were wary of endorsing another resolution. Republicans were especially reluctant because the 1968 campaign was relatively close. LBJ, for reasons of practical necessity, did not ask them for support; therefore, he did not risk the embarrassment of rejection.[78]

Nixon also was expressing his opinion during the spring of 1967. After spending three days in Vietnam for conferences and briefings, as part of a month-long Asian tour, he claimed critical Democrats were a "major factor" in prolonging the war. He would not, when questioned by reporters, discuss his policy differences with the administration until he returned home.[79] Nixon did indicate several days later that he would recommend an increased effort to secure victory through bombing or mining Haiphong's harbor and support further attempts to improve the pacification program upon which he did not elaborate. Nixon, with effusive optimism, predicted, "It can be said now that the defeat of the Communist forces in South Vietnam is inevitable. The only question is, how soon?"[80]

Richard Nixon always has been one of this nation's prominent spokesmen on foreign affairs since the late 1940s. The aforementioned tour of Vietnam made him even more cognizant of America's position within the international community. He was quick to perceive the misconception about American power and the will to use it. After his Asian tour, he commented,

There is a monstrous myth abroad, created and believed by Hanoi, that the United States is so divided that they can win in Washington and the United States the victory they cannot win on the battlefield. If the people of the United States could realize that by uniting they can shorten the war and bring peace this would be more important than sending 1 million men to Vietnam.[81]

This statement is characteristically Nixon, but it also may help explain the Republican view on foreign policy. For many years Republicans had carefully measured their words and criticism when discussing war tactics in South Vietnam. Their position, at least in part, was a realization of the American position within the international community.

Despite the fact that Johnson was receiving Republican support, no matter how cautious or nourishing, several Republican senators were searching out ways to form a new party consensus on Vietnam. At a luncheon held sometime during late March, or early

April, Jacob Javits, Charles Percy, and Margaret Chase Smith from
Maine met to chart a new course away from administration policy
on the Vietnam War. Previously, the president had encouraged
senators to speak privately with him about their reservations on
the war; therefore, the dissent remained private and no extra fuel
was added to the public criticism.[82] This tactic also allowed for no
outward display of disunity. But some members of the United
States Senate were becoming restive—which was not surprising,
considering the national mood at the time—and the luncheon held
that spring resulted in publication of a report entitled, "The War
in Vietnam." Issued under the auspices of the Senate Policy Committee on May 1, 1967, the report was similar in nature to the
documents released by House Republicans. The Senate narrative
reviewed American policy towards Indochina since World War II,
but it lacked any substantial alternatives to the current policy. However, it did ask Republicans to answer two fundamental questions:

(a) What precisely is our national interest in Thailand, Cambodia, Vietnam,
and Laos?

(b) What further lengths are we prepared to go in support of this interest?[83]

From a historical perspective this report sought to clarify the
American involvement from Eisenhower to Johnson. In its conclusion, the report recognized the complexity of events within Asia
and Vietnam in particular. It noted the vast internal differences in
the political structures, religious variations, and philosophical attitudes in Vietnam. Finally, the report listed basic statements of
party philosophy to be aired for public consumption.

1. Does the Republican Party serve America best by saying that politics
   stops at the water's edge? That we must rally behind the President?
   Does bipartisanship mean that Democrat mistakes are Republican
   responsibilities?

2. Republicans—for two decades—have believed the United States must
   not become involved in a land war on the Asian continent. We are so
   involved today.

3. Republicans have believed that no American military intervention should
   be unilateral. Our commitment today in Vietnam is primarily unilateral.

4. Republicans, in 1954, made a limited commitment to the South Vietnam
   Government. Under the Democrats, our commitment has become open-
   ended.[84]

The paper was written by the policy committee staff and was
not intended for publication; rather, as one author has noted, it was
prepared for "confidential consideration by Republican Senators."[85]
The contents of this document were highly controversial since it
illustrated a movement away from the Republican support that
Johnson had come to expect. Direct criticism was leveled on the
military conduct of the war and an objection was made to the
president's claim that his policies could be traced back to Eisenhower. Walter Zelman, who did an extensive review of the Senate's
feelings on Vietnam from 1964 to 1968, has written:

From the point of view of impartial political analysis the Republican White
Paper left much to be desired; it completely omitted the fact that Eisenhower was prepared to intervene militarily in Indochina in 1954; it did not
acknowledge the fact that it had been the Republicans, not the Democrats,
who had given President Johnson his strongest support on Vietnam policy;
it did acknowledge that its objections to Johnson's Vietnam policy
(with the exception of the references to Eisenhower) bore much greater
resemblances to statements of the Democratic doves than to anything
Republicans (with a few exceptions) had said in the past seven years.[86]

The policy report divided, rather than consolidated, the GOP on
war policy. Senator George Aiken of Vermont agreed that an honorable end to the war was desirable but not attainable since Johnson
predicated peace upon the idea of enemy capitulation.[87] Edward
Brooke aligned himself with Senate liberals when he agreed that
Johnson's efforts to bring Hanoi to the peace table would fail.[88]
Even Laird, as chairman of the House conference, noted the controversy caused by this Senate report. The dissension, according
to Laird, came primarily from Dirksen, who believed that Johnson
should be supported. Laird further stated that Dirksen felt Congress
could not run foreign affairs and Republicans would only hurt
themselves if they became all-out critics.[89] Not wanting to fall into
the trap, Senators Javits, Scott, and Percy issued a statement in
support of our commitment to keep South Vietnam free, but they

did not want to see a widened war which might bring in Communist Chinese intervention.[90]

Dirksen disagreed with those who issued unfavorable comment
on the report and sought to control the damage. He described it as
"complete," "authentic," and a "well-documented" overview of
past Republican positions and options which the GOP could consider in the future. According to the minority leader:

[It] makes no suggestion that (1) we modify our support of the President,
(2) that we increase or diminish our troop strength, (3) that we escalate or
de-escalate the conduct of the war, (4) that we retreat or withdraw, (5)
that we disavow our obligations under the SEATO treaty, (6) that we
pressure Vietnam into a course of action which it might be reluctant to
take.

He further stated:

Preserving wholly the right of full and fair inquiry and criticism, we
reiterate our wholehearted support of the Commander in Chief of our
armed forces. We reaffirm our position standing four-square behind him
and our field, air and sea commanders in Southeast Asia.[91]

Even Ford joined the bandwagon and supported his counterpart
in the Senate. He claimed "overwhelming" support of House Republicans to fight communism in Vietnam. He also did not want
the war to become a campaign issue but saw the possibility that
the people would make it one. Ford also noted that Republicans
did not make all the tactical decisions; therefore, questions could
be expected. The House minority leader also clarified his future
role by saying, "President Johnson is commander-in-chief. I did
not elect him. I tried to defeat him. I will try to defeat him again
in 1968. But on the issue of our country meeting the challenge, we
had better, as a nation, continue doing just that."[92]

All of this hoopla was more of just a passing interest to Lyndon
Johnson. During a news conference at the White House on May 3,
1967, he was asked if he had any views on the Senate Policy Report.
His answer was as follows:

I haven't read the details of the Senate Republican leader's statement. I
do not find myself in very much disagreement generally with him on these

matters. I think he is better able to express the Republican position in the Senate than I am.

What I have observed of his statements I am in general agreement with. I do not know what Senators, if any, are tied to this document. It looks kind of like—well, I don't know.[93]

Dirksen knew where the report emanated from and he knew who was tied with it, and he knew what had to be done with it. During a May luncheon at the Senate Republican Policy Committee, the report was shelved and not discussed. That same day, Dirksen held a news conference and his whip, Thomas Kuchel, repeated the bipartisan claim that the "Republican party should maintain bipartisan support of United States policy in Vietnam and should not use the Vietnam issue to gain possession of the White House in 1968." In short, Vietnam had to be concluded "honorably." At this juncture, Dirksen spoke up and claimed the policy committee report had been nothing more than a "historical document" and if it were to be published it would be all right for use in high school.[94]

These attempts at disavowal and denigration of the study were indicative of how Republican solidarity was unraveling on Capitol Hill; the Senate was especially hard hit. The Senate report had been shelved ostensibly in the interests of bipartisanship, but numerous Republicans (like Ford) reiterated the need for unrestricted bombing. Johnson did ease some of the restrictions for areas like Haiphong and Hanoi, but this did not quell the Republican disenchantment with his policies. Clearly, the GOP on Capitol Hill was moving towards a polarization between hawks and doves.

This shift became glaring as Charles Percy spoke before a group in Cincinnati during mid-August and assailed Johnson for "sucking us deeper and deeper into Southeast Asia." Percy advocated an honorable solution be achieved by 1968 which left Johnson room to bargain, but he introduced a theme which would be trumpeted by both parties in the future. "We have our battles to fight in our own country, battles against poverty and hunger and ignorance, battles for justice and equality."[95] Another senator, evoking a similar theme, was Mark Hatfield of Oregon, who advocated that Republicans be the "peace party" in 1968. He called the nation to "de-Americanize the whole Vietnam War," and he "favored halting the bombing of North Vietnam and a policy of de-escalation."[96] Of course, Johnson took the opposite approach, but these statements did indicate the Senate's growing unhappiness.

The increased bombing activity over North Vietnam by midsummer evidently spurred a frustrated group of House liberals to propose a de-escalation plan. A resolution drafted by Republicans Paul Findley of Illinois and F. Bradford Morse of Massachusetts was designed to have sixty-day bombing halts at a specified parallel on the map. Then the bombing would be stopped north of each parallel until reaching the border between North and South Vietnam. The Communist concession here was to have been a cessation of supply movements into the south, no more terrorist activities in that region, and release of American prisoners of war.[97] Although this move did not receive backing from Republican leaders, it did reveal the frustration felt by some congressmen over the war and its direction for the future.

One day after the Findley-Morse Resolution was introduced, Romney also called for a de-escalation of the bombing. Previously, he had backed Johnson on this military maneuver but was compelled to retreat from that position. In his judgment, quite different from Nixon's several months earlier, the Michigan Republican saw chances for an enlarged war with involvement by the Soviets and Chinese.[98] In a similar vein, during August, Romney declared peace as the GOP objective for 1968. This was the strongest indication from a possible presidential contender that negotiations may have been the path to follow.[99] At this point his prospects for a successful run at the Republican nomination seemed bright; during September, a Detroit television interview caught him off guard. Romney charged that the generals and diplomatic corps had "brainwashed" him about Vietnam and he adopted a truly pacifist stance when he said, "I no longer believe that it was necessary for us to get involved in South Vietnam to stop Communist aggression in Southeast Asia and to prevent Chinese Communist domination of Southeast Asia."[100] Romney undercut himself further when he remarked that Eisenhower never would have taken us this far militarily. The message was clear: we were too deeply entrenched with an Asian war. The comment about indoctrination was akin to a self-inflicted wound—even though it may have been a correct charge—and his statement haunted his aspirations for the Oval Office.

As fall approached, the cauldron of Vietnam was boiling. Potential overflows from this kettle grew as each week passed. Dirksen had staked out his territory on numerous occasions, but he gave very unequivocal support to LBJ and the Vietnam War. Questioned on the television program "Face the Nation," he gave his views forcefully on the president and the war:

> I have supported the President. I go on the theory that in his corner he has the Chiefs of Staff, he has the best military talent we have, he has these reports from Vietnam, probably every hour on the hour. And obviously he is in a better position to know about what the situation is than a layman back here 12,000 miles from the scene of operations who has not been to Vietnam in a long time, and who is in no position to judge.[101]

Keeping Dirksen's position in mind, it is interesting to see how a curious set of circumstances began unfolding during September and October. Thruston Morton, Republican senator from Kentucky, former Republican national chairman, and a political power in his own right, gave a stirring speech during late September charging that Lyndon Johnson had been duped by America's military-industrial complex into believing that military victory was attainable in Vietnam. Morton claimed he had been misled, too, and called for an end to bombing North Vietnam. The speech had a considerable impact upon the Senate since Morton had originally supported the president and was a "highly respected 'establishment' Senator, whose dissent might well represent . . . a considerable unrest amongst other moderate, and heretofore silent Senators."[102] Morton explained his change of heart by reflecting, "Actually I was troubled long before I made that speech, for at least several months. I'd found out that when you want to get something heard you have to do it strong, otherwise I wouldn't make the want ads."[103]

Given this backdrop, an acrimonious debate took place between Fulbright and Dirksen on October 3. For almost two hours they clashed head-on over the Vietnam War. Dirksen assumed what the *New York Times* later called "defender of Administration policy."[104] However, rumors ran rampant that Dirksen had taken to the Senate floor in order to quell a rebellion which seemed to be breaking out within Republican ranks over Vietnam.

There may have been a second reason for Dirksen's fiery oratory.

Media sources were circulating reports that he was fighting to retain his position as minority leader; the challenge came from Morton. During the debate with Fulbright, Dirksen vehemently stated that Vietnam was "our outside security line." If we lost the war, "our security line will run from Alaska to Hawaii." He remarked further, "I wasn't made a Senator to liquidate the holy fabric of freedom."[105] Dirksen's basic premise was that Marxism threatened stable world order and American blood shed in Vietnam helped prevent such a force from expanding. But when Thruston Morton entered the fight and criticized Johnson a second time, Dirksen shot back at him with a stinging critique.

It don't [*sic*] sound good and it don't look good. Have you heard the British demean their king or queen?

You don't demean the ruler—the President is not our ruler—but you don't demean him in the eyes of the people abroad, because when you do you demean the prestige of this republic, and I don't mean to do it.[106]

Of course, Dirksen had never denigrated Johnson in any form. Their friendship went back too far, spanned many congressional fights, and transcended political boundaries. In the eyes of many, Dirksen had become the president's chief defender on Capitol Hill. Throughout the years, though, he had carefully gauged his support—measured only as a true politician can. Speculation and rumor flowed even faster about the LBJ-Dirksen relationship after Dirksen received the William J. Donovan (of World War II and Office of Strategic Services fame) Medal at a banquet in Washington. Lyndon Johnson made an unexpected appearance and praised the senator. He claimed Dirksen had been referred to as a "fifth column" on Capitol Hill, which the *New York Times* said was "an allusion to their personal friendship which has caused discontent among both Republicans and Democrats."[107]

It was no surprise, then, that Johnson's Republican support was starting to wane. Senator Javits wanted the Senate to adopt a resolution that·would have circumvented the Gulf of Tonkin Resolution. This would have avoided embarrassing Johnson if the Tonkin Gulf had been repealed, voiced some sort of support for the president, but also narrowed the scope and authority originally granted during 1964.[108] Javits' idea pleased neither the hawks nor the doves.

While some thought it might serve to strengthen Johnson's hand, others saw political consequences and an erosion of national security interests. Filibusters were rarely considered as a form of protest since such actions might have an adverse political effect and harm men in the field.[109] Besides, those who dissented usually had access to administration officials, and Republicans such as Cooper and Aiken had considerable access due to their length of service and the personal respect that they commanded as Senators. Also, numerous senators expressed their feelings during executive sessions of the Senate Foreign Relations Committee.

This growing debate and restlessness in Congress over war policy was accentuated and sharpened by public criticism which grew increasingly militant. During October, numerous marches were held in the United States and other areas overseas to protest American war policy. The joint leadership, through a press conference statement dated October 26, 1967, expressed concern over the public demonstrations in Washington and around the nation. Recognizing the importance of historical dissent, and its tradition within American history, Ford and Dirksen embraced the concept of "unlimited criticism—in time of war and in time of peace" and felt this should be allowed. However, the congressional leaders argued that only a minority was complaining; therefore, this group "must be held in check hereafter and, when necessary, be brought to justice, legally but firmly by the scruff of their collective necks. The safety and the peace of mind of all decent, hard-working, law-abiding millions of other Americans *must* be preserved."[110] Implicit in this statement was the idea that most people supported the war. Those protesting did not make up the "silent majority" which Richard Nixon would reach out for a few years hence. The leadership's statement belied the fact that even Republicans were having problems and serious questions about our role in Vietnam, and many of them were decent, hard-working, law-abiding citizens who paid their taxes; some were even members of Congress.

As the first session of the Ninetieth Congress adjourned, Ford and Dirksen issued a report in early December 1967 entitled "The State of the Congress." Everett Dirksen gave assurances that our forces in Southeast Asia had full support of the minority party in Congress. He acknowledged executive control over the war and noted that many people sought solutions different from the administration's, but those differences needed to be conducted in an "orderly manner." In the year-end report he also questioned Johnson's guns-and-butter approach for the nation:

The State of the Congress today is one of vexation and deep-seated concern as we look about us here at home. We see an Administration wholly blind in its belief that the enormous costs of the war in Vietnam can and will be borne by our people while at the same time the Administration seeks unrestrained license to promote and finance multi-billion dollar social programs.

Dirksen was now beginning to tie domestic and foreign policy into one bundle. Ford carried the argument further by demanding the following:

Insistence that this Administration, to the extent that it may still be able to do so, succeed in Viet Nam or be prepared to yield to a Republican Administration whose new direction, new ideas and new vigor might well offer our people and the world a more probable prospect of peace.

Insistence upon the immediate establishment of a bipartisan blue ribbon commission of America's best experts to re-examine our short and long-range defense posture in this time of national peril.[111]

Eight days later, Dirksen issued a separate statement entitled " 'Quo Vadis?' Whither America?" which, in effect, said what next America? He argued, first and foremost, that we must always give high priority to Europe with reference to our foreign policy. He noted the stakes were increasing every day in Vietnam as the casualties rose, financial cost of combat escalated, and the unpopularity of the war intensified domestically. In Dirksen's words: "[T]here is little evident reason to hope for victory in the foreseeable future." A further elaboration indicated a genuine fear, a perception if you will, that we faced more than a challenge overseas.

[A]s America's expenditure of blood and of treasure continues unabated, the Communists—Red and Yellow—conspire without respite to undermine us at home and abroad to do all that may yet, they believe, achieve their dominance of us and the destruction of free America.[112]

Party leaders such as Nixon were also becoming more vocal. Nixon urged that the Vietnam War be brought to a successful conclusion since LBJ had failed to communicate the "fundamental strategic importance of Vietnam" to the public. Nixon observed that if we lost the war it would be a "reward for aggression" and serve only to encourage other "wars of liberation."[113] The Republican theory was clear: stiff resistance of the Marxist challenge served to modify Communist moves. Europe served as an example of how the containment policy had worked; now Asia was the next step.

George Romney was still trying to carve out his niche in terms of Republican politics and a stand on Vietnam. His wavering displayed an uncertainty that did not serve him as he sought to move into the forefront of presidential politics. During early November, he suggested a neutralization of those nations in Asia directly involved with the war but offered no specific details. Romney announced his candidacy during November and took a tour of the Soviet Union the following month. While speaking with Soviet leaders at the Kremlin, he broached the subject of neutralization and was told it might be discussed if the bombing of North Vietnam ceased. For two hours he spoke with Soviet Premier Alexei Kosygin in order to gauge more completely the Russian attitude on America's involvement with Asia and his neutralization proposal. According to Romney, Kosygin "made it quite clear to me during the course of our discussion they would never let us win in North Vietnam." He further noted that Kosygin warned the Soviets would also "start diversionary troubles elsewhere, if necessary, including the Middle East."[114]

The political winds were blowing, of course, and Republicans were hoping to capture the White House. Dirksen and Ford even went so far as to suggest, in a December news conference, that a Republican president might not be as constrained in his approaches to peace talks or negotiated settlements. Dirksen repeated the belief that "only the president" had the information and responsibility for guiding the war. He further chided Johnson with this statement:

The Congress and the people have seen all too little evidence of genuine effort to explore and exploit the diplomatic opportunities available to us in this regard. Channels of diplomacy, economic and otherwise, still remain open for our use.[115]

Ford backed up Dirksen with the following analogy. Republicans, according to the House minority leader, could gain peace with "less hindrances of the past—a new President not locked into the position this Administration has been forced to put itself—just as President Eisenhower brought peace to South Korea."[116] But Dirksen could not resist the political stab at North Vietnam's leader when he said, "If Ho Chi Minh doesn't know by now he's not going to do better under a Republican Administration, he'll find out the hard way."[117]

On a similar approach was Eisenhower, who began to become more vocal about his views on Vietnam. Joined by General Omar Bradley in a televised interview, the two military men were questioned about the war's strategy by moderator Harry Reasoner. Neither general accepted the privileged sanctuary concept which allowed Communist forces to escape into neighboring nations with no fear of retaliation. Bradley and Eisenhower advocated hot pursuit on the ground or by air.[118] The following day Nixon declared Eisenhower's view as correct from a military standpoint. However, he argued that it was unsound diplomatically and politically because the ground war could be possibly widened. In effect, diplomacy took precedence over military movements at that particular point.[119]

Throughout most of the 1960s, Eisenhower had made very few public comments about the conduct of American foreign policy. During a pre-Christmas interview in 1967, he gave his views on the forthcoming presidential election, less than a year away. His stand on Vietnam was very forceful.

I don't regard myself as a missionary, and I don't want to convert anybody.

But if any Republican or Democrat suggests that we pull out of Vietnam and turn our backs on the more than 13,000 Americans who died in the cause of freedom there, they will have me to contend with.

That's one of the few things that would start me off on a series of stump speeches across the nation.[120]

The inferences, or suggestions, flowing through December were numerous. They ranged from the belief that a Republican administration could solve the problem of Vietnam to a concern over extensive financial expenditures at home and abroad, internal dissent against the war, and a claim of internal and external subversion of American interests. Presidential politics, too, were coming on stage; within a short time the American landscape would be covered with aspirants, and national attention would be focused on the ritual of a general election.

THE CHANGING FORTUNES OF WAR AND POLITICS: 1968

The campaign of 1968 was ushered in by more than just a growing American military presence in Vietnam. Despite troop levels of nearly a half-million men, domestic and military aid to the Republic of Vietnam running into the billions, there was an uncertainty in American society. Lyndon Johnson's cause and America's crusade was bogged down in an Asian land war with no end in sight. Republicans sensed a political victory for themselves as the fall election approached. But Vietnam had become more than just an Asian war; it was also a domestic political problem with numerous dimensions. Other forces, of a profound nature, pulled at the very fabric of the society. Hate, violence, political assassinations, racial tensions, and war protests in the streets were all indicative of passions out of control. Even though these extra dimensions were important, the single, most pressing issue of the day was Vietnam.

Part of the groundwork for a Republican victory in 1968 came from several quarters. As early as November 1967, the Republican Coordinating Committee had compiled a study entitled "The American Image Abroad." The gist of this evaluation was that our role as a major international power was in question by other nations. The study advocated more development in areas of political communications such as broadcasts through the Voice of America. The theory was that by conducting this kind of public relations, other nations would be able to understand us and then more easily relate to our message of democracy. This approach was significant since it reflected the Republican preoccupation with our position in the world. But the power for Republican, and American, direction, change, renewal, and reformation still emanated from Capitol Hill.

Once again Ford and Dirksen led their party from a national forum. During an interview on January 14, 1968, Dirksen stated that he still supported Johnson's policy of fighting Communist aggression in Vietnam, but the senator still wanted to "criticize the methods." In the same interview, though, he outlined what was

to become the classic Republican frustration during 1968 in relation
to the Vietnam War. "What are we going to do other than what
the President is doing right now? We can't retreat, we can't pull
out and we can't get the other side to negotiate."[121]

On January 23, 1968, the GOP responded once again to Johnson's
State of the Union Address. The response, however, was staged
much differently than in the past. Elaborate preparations preceded
the television show as the joint leadership held at least three meetings prior to the nationwide broadcast. Senator George Murphy of
California was in charge of arrangements, and his Hollywood background with film productions proved helpful. Murphy suggested
that the program be live, with a master of ceremonies and three
podiums. During the first half of the broadcast, the emcee would
switch between Dirksen and Ford with questions and the congressional leaders responding. He also speculated that the second half
of the show should "use four of the best-looking Senators and four
Congressmen."[122] In the end, Murphy was the master of ceremonies, but the minutes from a joint leadership meeting in January
indicate that Dirksen would cover international affairs and Ford the
domestic issues. All of this elaborate preparation, consultation, and
the business of image coincided with newspaper reports that some
members of the GOP were complaining that the Dirksen-Ford team
had lost its effectiveness; therefore, new faces were added to bolster
the Republican image on television. Melvin Laird claims this overall
image problem was untrue but has agreed that new faces were
needed. For instance, as Laird has noted, George Bush was a fresh-
man congressman from Texas and, since LBJ was from Texas,
Republicans thought it might be a nice touch to have a younger
man on television, especially one from the Lone Star State.[123]

Senator John Tower, another Texan, was chosen to speak. According to Tower, the entire Republican group of speakers was
selected because of its competence in key areas, and he believes it
was a collective decision made by Ford and Dirksen to structure
the program in the way it was eventually presented.[124] During his
program segment, Tower called on the United States to utilize its
military superiority and end what he termed "a self-defeating policy
of gradualism." Tower believed he spoke with some authority on
that need for change since he had made two trips to Vietnam. Tower
has argued that we had North Vietnam, in his phrase, "on the

ropes"; that fact was supported by a friend of the senator, John Cauldron, who was the British consulate general in Hanoi. According to Tower, we should have stepped up the bombings and used "unrelenting pressure." Instead, we eased off, gave North Vietnam a chance to recoup, and encouraged their will to fight.[125]

The other Republican speakers during this televised event called for unification on America's stand in Vietnam, but these views were not indicative of all party members, not even the majority. But Senators John Sherman Cooper and Jacob Javits readily agreed that their colleagues' statements did not illustrate the major elements of Republican thought. The problem was that the GOP was divided between some sort of negotiated settlement and some form of military victory through the use of increased firepower belonging to the United States. All of this rhetoric belied the fact that Republicans did not control the military machinery, but they set out to gain the office which did during the spring of 1968.

The season of spring primaries put Republicans in an awkward position. To attack Democratic policies on Vietnam was one thing, but offering solutions on how the war might be concluded successfully was another matter. The GOP never missed an opportunity to exploit divisions on the other side of the aisle; however, Republicans tried to remain flexible so their position to criticize would not be destroyed if the war ended.[126]

The Tet Offensive during late January 1968 shattered the administration's claim that the war was going to be won. Communist raiders had entered Saigon and laid seige to the American embassy; other cities in South Vietnam also were attacked. After Tet, sentiment in the Senate for peace began to shift. Those who had supported the war, or at least refrained from sharp public criticism, reached the conclusion that our policy in Vietnam was not reaching the desired ends. Others, who were long-standing critics of America's role in South Vietnam, grew more vociferous in their dissent. The conclusion was that no further escalation was desirable; America's efforts were to be geared for withdrawal.[127]

Three Republicans sought their party's nomination during the spring primaries of 1968. As noted earlier, Romney was the first to announce his intentions during late 1967. His peace plan, outlined the previous spring, was denigrated because his brainwashing statement became imprinted upon the public perception. The Michigan governor did, however, give some additional criteria for his peace initiative during the spring campaign. Returning from overseas in early January, Romney characterized his recent trip to South Vietnam as beneficial; during the last visit, he had been duped. In his judgment, our foreign policy had to be recast through a recommitment of our resources and definite outlines of our national goals. This type of action would inspire confidence from other nations, thereby creating more worldwide support for the United States.[128]

On January 15, 1968, Romney unveiled his neutralization plan for Southeast Asia prior to the New Hampshire primary. The essentials of the program were as follows: (1) removal of all foreign troops and bases, (2) no alliances by nations of this area with those from outside the region, (3) self-determination for the nations of Southeast Asia, and (4) economic development of the entire region. For Vietnam he urged formation of a coalition government for all factions, a cease-fire on all sides, and amnesty for those who had fought against the South. He also proposed that the Vietcong was to renounce terror and coercion. Departing from his prepared text, Romney commented that he refused "to support an Administration that cannot wage the conflict effectively or seek peace convincingly." Finally, Romney urged international supervision of the area under the auspices of the United Nations.[129]

Romney's blueprint was geared towards a de-escalation of the war. A few days prior to releasing his peace plan, the governor decried a bombing pause unless there was some basis for a settlement. He also noted this would be his position during the campaign.[130] But Romney had another reason for advocating his program. He saw Vietnam in the context of a superpower confrontation. Since he had announced his candidacy first, the onus for some sort of plan—peace or war—was upon him. Between April 1967 and January 1968, he opted for a peace plan, yet wavered on whether or not bombing of North Vietnam was to continue. In the end, his campaign floundered and he was the first man out of the Republican column in 1968.

Rockefeller, who had stood in the shadows for months on his candidacy for the White House, announced he would accept a draft at the national convention. However, he made it clear that he would not criticize Johnson on his prosecution of the war.[131] During the latter part of 1967 and early 1968, Rockefeller had not addressed himself to Vietnam as a political issue. On April 30, he announced his candidacy and tried to gain the momentum needed for primary wins as opposed to a convention draft. During one campaign stop, he defined his view of an honorable settlement in Vietnam. The answer was elusive when he said "that the people of South Vietnam have the opportunity of self-determination" in connection with the establishment of their own government.[132] Rockefeller's late start, lack of an adequate staff, and distrust of many conservative Republicans kept him from gaining the nomination.[133] Hoping beyond reality that Nixon's convention lead would erode, Rockefeller was faced with the Herculean task of wresting the nomination from Nixon. It could not be done.

Three weeks prior to the Republican National Convention, Rockefeller proposed a four-stage plan to end the war in Vietnam. He claimed Lyndon Johnson had not "created the atmosphere of mutual confidence that is essential to success" for the peace talks. The New York governor's proposal was similar to Romney's in that it called for a gradual military pull back on both sides, creation of a neutral buffer force to keep the warring armies separate, and participation by the Vietcong in elections. Also, North Vietnam would fall back to the demilitarized zone between both nations. The presence of a neutral peacekeeping force from other nations would patrol the region and eventually all foreign troops would be removed. Free elections were to be held under international supervision and eventually North and South Vietnam would decide whether they wished to unify. If this was their choice, the peacekeeping force would be removed.[134] The plan failed to capture the nation's imagination and the allegiance of Republican delegates at the convention. Rockefeller and Romney ended on deflated notes; Nixon, conversely, came out on top without proposing anything of substance for ending the war.

Nixon began forming his strategy for capturing the Republican nomination years before announcing his formal candidacy on February 1, 1968. This long familiar face in Republican circles was reemerging—like a Phoenix from its ashes—and he began preparation for this move by organizing a formal staff to direct his nomination effort in January 1967. The entire movement, however, was very low key.[135]

When it came to the Vietnam War, Nixon essentially refused to give any details of a plan concerning an end to the conflict, or even a victory, and on numerous occasions stated that the Johnson administration should not be undercut while it negotiated a peace settlement. Labeling his plan as "secret," Nixon was almost exempt from questions on how he would handle the fighting overseas. He openly advocated the principle that Lyndon Johnson and Dean Rusk were to receive wider latitude for their negotiations. Under no circumstances did Nixon want to be viewed as the "spoiler" in the quest for peace. Ironically, and understandably, deep schisms over Johnson's policies ripped the Democratic party to shreds. This was a cleavage so deep it spawned serious dovish contenders such as Senators Eugene McCarthy from Minnesota and Robert Kennedy from New York. Johnson was so beleaguered by internal party strife and nationwide dissent he chose not to seek renomination and withdrew from the race on March 31.

Johnson's withdrawal from the political fight cost him a precious ally. Eisenhower had counseled LBJ on numerous occasions about war policy, but at the same time the former president was being used for purposes of support and bipartisan unity. By September 1966, Eisenhower was becoming disenchanted over Johnson's war strategy. He disliked the gradualism and believed too many decisions were centralized within the administration, thereby keeping field commanders from the freedom they required to fight the war effectively. Eisenhower also was concerned about the duration of this conflict and the possible disappearance of public support. By July 1967, he was so frustrated he publicly called for a congressional declaration of war. The increased public dissent and rebellion, in his view, was bordering on treason. The final straw for Eisenhower, however, came in February and March 1968. Johnson came to visit his predecessor in Palm Desert, California, and promised to persevere with the goal of victory in Vietnam. However, after the Tet Offensive, LBJ put a ceiling on troop reinforcements and then withdrew from the race in March. According to Stephen Ambrose, "Eisenhower was livid with anger, his remarks about Johnson's cutting and running unprintable. Goodpaster (the White House liaison), went on to a new assignment, and Eisenhower's connection with the Johnson Administration came to an end."[136]

Throughout the late winter and spring of 1968, Richard Nixon walked a tightrope. He stated early on that Johnson should not cease bombing North Vietnam because there was always a renewed Communist offensive in the south shortly thereafter. According to Nixon, the way to convince Hanoi that peace was in their interest was to "prosecute the war more effectively." Therefore, he reiterated his commitment to the objective but not the method.[137] Some reporters who followed Nixon during this period were convinced his subsequent positions on Vietnam were developed on the campaign trail. Nixon wished to bring the war to a successful conclusion and use diplomatic moves in the future to insure that the situation would not be repeated.[138]

In early March, Nixon pledged to end the war but he never said what means were to be used. With this one campaign statement he commented on the present frustration yet looked to the future:

> If in November this war is not over, after all this power has been at their disposal, then I say the American people will be justified to elect the new leadership. And I pledge to you the new leadership will end the war and win the peace in the Pacific—and that is what America wants.[139]

At this juncture he criticized Johnson without naming him, because the president had not used the military power at his disposal. Nixon recognized the inherent frustration among the people who were seeking—he hoped—new leadership for an end to this war. Then he pledged the new leadership would end the war; and bring peace to the Pacific area since Americans wanted the matter settled. Consequently, his theme was simple and yet complex in its structure.

Throughout March, Nixon refused to reveal his plan for ending the war on the premise that if he became president it would weaken his bargaining position. He did not want to adopt a definitive posture, and yet he proclaimed that a Republican administration could reach a settlement.[140] Towards the end of March, Nixon's aides were sensitive to newspaper reports that he would not reveal his plan. The generalities, according to the *New York Times*, troubled Rockefeller so much that he became contemptuous of Nixon. In Rockefeller's view, why keep a plan secret when hundreds die each week?[141] But Nixon was the master of political negotiators. While on the campaign trail through Indiana for its primary, he argued that a presidential candidate should not have been speaking out on the war since such actions would only jeopardize chances for peace.

He said, "In my view, no Presidential candidate—of either party— should say anything or do anything to destroy the fragile hope that has arisen today."[142] Politically and realistically, the GOP had not made the major policy decisions on a land war in Asia and from a public perception, Vietnam may have been easily viewed as a "Democratic War." Therefore, the best strategy for the loyal opposition was to be just that: loyal. A low profile was to be the essence of victory in November. Nor could Republicans change the way Johnson prosecuted the war, no matter what plan they advocated.

Even the joint leadership muted some of its criticism in the area of foreign affairs during the spring and summer of 1968. Dirksen and Ford continued their tradition of making public statements via press conferences, but they usually refrained from harsh statements even though earlier in the year Dirksen publicly expressed doubt as to whether the administration could end the war. What seems even more significant, however, was Dirksen's neglect in even mentioning Vietnam during July 1968 when he reviewed foreign policy concerns during a press conference. It is possible he wished to leave all this business alone until after the Republican National Convention since a statement would have to be made about foreign policy by this group.

Miami Beach was the site for the twenty-ninth Republican National Convention. The formal meeting ran from August 5 to 8, but a platform was forged ahead of time, and one of the planks covered Vietnam. Party planners had made a concerted effort in the spring to lay the foundation for a concise statement concerning America's role in international affairs. The genesis for the foreign affairs section of the platform came from the Republican Coordinating Committee's publication entitled *Choice for America*. On April 17, the coordinating committee released its position paper on the strategic role of America's military forces. Prepared in March, and circulated to Nixon and Eisenhower for their review prior to final release, the paper criticized Johnson on his use of gradualism in Vietnam. This was the first major statement about Vietnam to emanate from the committee since 1965 and the first paper to evolve from the newly formed Republican group on national security.[143]

Another committee article which appeared in May of 1968 was entitled "Democratic Foreign Policy: The Crisis of Confidence" and gave an overview of American participation within the international community. The thrust of this synopsis centered on the following areas: (1) our alliances were almost non-existent, (2) our strategic superiority had fallen behind, and (3) we had allowed ourselves to pursue nonessential objectives in foreign affairs. While praising the Eisenhower years as a period of strength and stability, the Democratic administrations of the 1960s were castigated for being soft on communism. In a self-serving statement the report argued:

Only because the previous Republican Administration had bequeathed to its successors a coherent body of foreign policy based upon unrivaled diplomatic, military and economic strength, were the Democrats able to improvise and experiment for so long without having to account for their errors. Slow as the day of reckoning has been in arriving, it is now clearly at hand. We see it in the tragic loss of America's stature in the world.[144]

The committee report further stated that the desire to end the arms race was a neutral concern with Democrats. "But there was a critical difference in the basic approach: in all negotiations Republicans required the Communists to meet us half-way."[145]

In terms of Vietnam, the document claimed Republicans had left Asia "in relative peace." The main obstacle to a truce in this region was the Soviets and Chinese since they were aiding North Vietnam. Even though this document was critical of the opposition party, Republicans wished Johnson well in his diplomatic initiatives.

We support his declared objective of an honorable peace, one that would rule out a Communist take-over. Acceptance of a settlement lacking proper safeguards would betray our allies and the South Vietnamese people. It would be an outrage in light of the sacrifices made by our men—living and dead.[146]

Gerald Ford was selected as the permanent chairman of the Republican National Convention in 1968. Ford has explained how a platform was formulated and eventually accepted. The National Committee established a small group which wrote the draft. It was then circulated to the party leadership in Congress and the presidential candidates where it was refined even more. The document then was reviewed by the party leaders in a nearly final form and went to the platform committee for more input. This process usually develops a fairly cohesive statement of party philosophy and goals which is accepted by the convention.[147] During the 1968 convention, Dirksen had a major role in formulating the Platform because he chaired the committee on resolutions which wrote the final document.

Dirksen made it clear that he had no intention of making the war a partisan issue. According to the New York Times, Dirksen even had the room swept for bugs since he believed the platform committee had been compromised in San Francisco in 1964.[148] A problem arose as the 102 members of the committee came to the convention with the impression that they would compose the platform but found a draft had already been prepared by Dirksen and a group of nine others.[149] Republican Senator Jack Miller of Iowa indicated that he would block any move that Dirksen made on a nonpartisan stand over Vietnam. Miller saw a deception on Johnson's part, and this deception had been at work during the past four years. Johnson had increased our involvement, sent more troops overseas, and so broadened the overall military commitment that we were doing most of the fighting. For Miller the situation was quite clear: "the prolonged war strategy with its resulting casualties should be laid at the doorstep of the Johnson Administration."[150]

Most party leaders, though, were urging their fellow Republicans to avoid bitter rancor, but a divergence of thought emerged between the liberal and conservative wings of the GOP. The two groups were probably best personified by two individuals: Ronald Reagan who sought the presidential nomination for himself and John Lindsay, the mayor of New York City. Reagan, during a convention speech, forcefully remarked, "It is time to tell friend and foe alike, we are in Vietnam because it is our national interest to be there." Lindsay, in his convention speech, countered with the belief that "the war in Vietnam has estranged the majority of the American people from their own Government. It has reduced our international prestige to the lowest point in modern history."[151] By August 3, the platform committee also was split between hawks and doves on the Vietnam plank. Nixon, speaking before the platform committee, urged that the war had to be ended. Until this happened the United States should be committed to a strategy which used "few men and at less cost." If we strengthened the South Vietnamese forces, we could phase out our troops. Nixon also lashed out at the fact that American military power had been squandered, the South Vietnamese were ill-prepared to defend themselves, and a new type of guerrilla warfare was needed which employed psychological, economic, and political dimensions. Finally, in Nixon's judgment, Johnson had not been candid with the American people and he had lost their confidence.[152]

Ronald Reagan also had his supporters at the convention, and he pressed for a hard-line statement endorsing America's commitment in Southeast Asia. Reagan was disturbed over Johnson's unwillingness to fight the war without winning it. By getting bogged down in an Asian land war, Johnson had committed a horrible error, and the only way to correct the problem was a significant increase of the bombing to destroy the enemy's power. He did not rule out nuclear weapons, but he did not advocate their use. What he preferred was to keep the North Vietnamese guessing as to whether we would use such force.[153]

Richard Nixon and Nelson Rockefeller joined forces to support a pro-peace plank, and Charles Goodell was the chief negotiator for Rockefeller's team. Each side took excerpts from their candidate's speeches, blended them together, and came up with a peace proposal. Goodell believes that Nixon's people accepted most of Rockefeller's proposals sensing the need for a common ground among the GOP.[154] The main points of this general agreement came out in the following manner with the platform:

Militarily, the Administration's piecemeal commitment of men and material has wasted our massive military superiority and frittered away our options. The result has been a prolonged war of attrition. Throughout this period the Administration has been slow in training and equipping South Vietnamese units both for fighting the war and for defending their country after the war is over.

We pledge to adopt a strategy relevant to the real problems of the war, concentrating of the security of the population, on developing a greater sense of nationhood, and strengthening the local forces. It will be a strategy permitting a progressive de-Americanization of the war, both military and civilian.

We pledge a program for peace in Vietnam—neither peace at any price nor a camouflaged surrender of legitimate United States or allied interests— but a positive program that will offer a fair and equitable settlement to all, based on the principle of self-determination, our national interests and the cause of long-range world peace.[155]

Nixon accepted a Vietnam plank that moved Republicans away from conflict overseas to one that called for negotiations over war in Asia. With the Republican course charted, Nixon became the presidential standard bearer and prepared to face-off against Hubert Humphrey in the fall campaign.

The congressional leadership also tried to stay within the parameters of the platform, and during a press conference Dirksen quoted from the platform and pledged "to dedicate our efforts toward the restoration of peace both at home and abroad."[156] A month later, Dirksen underscored the seriousness of America's domestic and international trouble by stating, "At war abroad, in turmoil at home, divided, uncertain, apprehensive, our people are in torment greater than any they have known since The War Between The States."[157]

During the fall campaign, Nixon remained fairly quiet about Vietnam. He had supported Johnson on several occasions and would not advocate de-escalation under the current circumstances. Nixon's low profile proved to be effective since the Democrats were falling apart as they divided over the war and their disastrous convention which had been held in Chicago. Nixon was silent not only because of peace negotiations, but he did not want to harm his bargaining position in January if he were to become president. The precedent for his actions went back to Eisenhower. Without a specific plan for ending the Korean War, Eisenhower had been able to negotiate an agreement once he entered office. Nixon wished to preserve his options, too, and this strategy worked to his advantage.[158]

For several months, the Johnson administration had been conducting peace negotiations with the North Vietnamese in Paris. By October, a breakthrough in the talks seemed imminent. This occurrence might have produced a shift in public sentiment, thereby helping Humphrey with the election. Nixon moved closer to the position that a bombing halt was acceptable if North Vietnam demonstrated a willingness to negotiate. By following this stance Nixon did not appear to be implacable in terms of peace negotiations.[159] On October 31, Johnson assembled the congressional leadership at the White House to announce that the bombing of North Vietnam would be halted and peace talks were to resume on November 6.

Neither Nixon nor Spiro Agnew, his vice presidential running mate, voiced much public comment on these peace negotiations. During an appearance at Madison Square Garden in New York City, before a crowd of nearly nineteen thousand partisans, Nixon pointed to Agnew on the stage behind him and remarked, "Neither he nor I will destroy the chance of peace. We want peace."[160] Nixon's low-key strategy on the issue of Vietnam was effective, and Republicans gained the White House after an eight-year absence. The victory, though, was in no way a landslide for a party so long removed from power.

5.

A LEGACY OF TRANSITION

When opportunities arose for input with foreign policy initiatives nearly three decades after World War II, Republicans were in an awkward position. Their minority status as the party out of power sapped their strength and will to deal aggressively with the new demands at the end of World War II. There are, however, reasons beyond the political statistics, and they can be viewed in five transitory stages during a thirty-year span.

The first was the isolationist stance that the GOP adopted from the 1930s and prior to the attack on Pearl Harbor. For the most part, Republicans did not wish the United States to meet foreign commitments; rather, the disillusionment from World War I, reparations failures, and a worldwide economic depression worked against a favorable climate for foreign entanglements. Pearl Harbor, of course, changed the direction for America's world role and the Republican viewpoint.

The second phase began in 1942, and once again Republicans had no basic control over the foreign policy apparatus. This condition remained through 1952, but World War II had removed the predominant isolationism from their ranks. Arthur Vandenberg emerged as the leading spokesman for his party and made a serious attempt to formulate a bipartisan tradition of stopping politics at the water's edge when dealing with foreign affairs. Although his vision was limited and bipartisanship was difficult to sustain after 1945, the concept increased Republican credibility for a restructuring of the postwar world. Vandenberg's death, the subsequent rise of Bob Taft, and the Korean War severely tested the bipartisan model. Republicans, as well as other Americans, were frustrated by developments during the early postwar period. The loss of mainland China to communism, a Korean stalemate, and a containment policy which supported wars of limited engagement, increased the frustration and disillusionment felt by so many people.

The third transition for the GOP began during 1953 with Eisenhower's administration. Eisenhower, representing the eastern wing of his party, shifted the GOP to a more moderate stance on foreign policy issues as opposed to the isolationism preferred by some. It must be remembered that the GOP had been out of the presidency for twenty years, and they had controlled Congress only twice during the same time period. Their absence in the White House forced Republican proposals and alternatives to be developed by the minority leadership on Capitol Hill. By not controlling the foreign policy mechanisms, Republicans were effectively out of the decision-making process. Their alternative was to criticize, but innovation was lacking. Even if they proposed a new program, for instance, there was no opportunity to test it, modify the idea, and start out again. This was one of the most serious drawbacks which Republicans had faced as the loyal opposition since World War II.

Eisenhower's ascendancy brought a rejuvenation to Republican politics. By forming America's foreign policy, Eisenhower took the leadership of his party while Halleck and Dirksen sought to keep their colleagues behind the president. This action gave them a foundation for the future. When Eisenhower left office in 1961, the foreign policy role for the Republican party then devolved upon the congressional leaders who performed their historical role of speaking for the loyal opposition. Eisenhower, sensing a need for continuity and still wishing to have input with his party's direction, orchestrated the creation of the joint Senate-House leadership prior to his departure from the White House.

The fourth phase was the joint leadership. The Republican minority position was consistently reinforced as they lost congressional races and two presidential bids during the 1960s. In the first instance, it was incumbent upon the GOP to challenge Kennedy, but a curious relationship existed between the new president and the Halleck-Dirksen team. Quite simply, they liked one another and respected each other as politicians. From our viewpoint today, it is literally true that the personalities meshed together in a unique fashion. There were, however, several common threads that help explain the relationship between these three men. They all had congressional experience and demonstrated a valid concern over communism, and they believed that Communism needed to be contained. Essentially, they were Cold War fighters. Their methodology for dealing with Communist containment differed somewhat. Even though Halleck and Dirksen used tough rhetoric, Kennedy knew he could count on them to work on behalf of the national interest. Perhaps it was an unwritten trust between them, but they knew when rhetoric had to cease and unity begin. In one sense, it could be argued they all practiced Vandenberg's doctrine of bipartisanship in a fitting manner. Kennedy also needed bipartisan support because of his narrow election victory in 1960. But the severe test was yet to come, because America's commitment to Vietnam was relatively small during the early 1960s.

With Dirksen and Halleck, words were more than symbolic. They took a harsh, pragmatic stand towards communism, but in the early stages of Kennedy's administration their criticism was directed towards the president's men. By 1962 the scenario changed, and in 1963 Republicans were positioning themselves for the upcoming national elections.

Barry Goldwater's devastating defeat in 1964 only added to the discord and confusion within the GOP. But this situation also led Republicans into their fifth and final transition, which included a party reorganization and creation of the coordinating committee. With Mel Laird as conference chairman and Gerald Ford as minority leader, House Republicans made some significant and dynamic changes in their area of government. All of these factors coalesced so that Republicans, at least in the House, moved to a period of critical thinking on Johnson and America's most pressing issue, the Vietnam War.

The House leadership's intent was to provide distinctive challenges to Johnson's policies and programs. The minority, however, faced an especially tough decision. How could they criticize the president about his Vietnam policy yet refrain from harming America's international position and its troops in the field? A partial answer came through challenging the policymakers (not always a direct attack upon the president) and demanding a military victory in Vietnam. However, the Republican leaders on all levels hesitated in their criticism to a certain extent because militant dissent was on the rise, especially during 1967 and 1968. The only real alternatives offered by Republicans were proper use of America's basic military strength and advocacy of a will to win. Republicans also were cognizant of the opportunity to capture the White House in 1968, and it was a political reality that could not be overlooked. Between 1961 and 1968 most members of the Republican party did not play "politics" with the war; consequently, they were usually quite supportive of the administration. This does not belie the fact that they wanted Johnson, or his potential successor, defeated, and, yes, they wanted to control Capitol Hill. But they were unwilling to risk a complete confrontation with the Democrats and the president. Their reasons range from philosophical, patriotic, and practical political considerations.

The favored goal in Asia was to keep South Vietnam free of Communist control. Republicans embraced this vision, offered support, and even criticized Democrats and dissidents for undermining the nation's position. It must be remembered, though, that the Vietnam experience was unique in American history. Korea, for example, was a shorter military engagement and therefore not as divisive as Vietnam. Republicans, and the nation, had never faced anything like the Vietnam War. Their minority political position reinforced the frustration. If the GOP had any quarrel, it arose over the military strategy. The bombing of strategic military targets in North Vietnam or the mining of Haiphong's Harbor would have quenched the Republican thirst for a more effective prosecution of the war. LBJ limited the commitment to an incremental level, which led to great anxiety not only for the nation but for the politicians, too. The series of incremental pressures upon North Vietnam failed to bring a victory in Southeast Asia, which was so eagerly sought by Republicans during the 1960s.

Besides the political approach of Republicans wishing to unseat Johnson and patriotic questions of dissent, the philosophical dimension about the minority party's role during the postwar period remains somewhat vague. Between 1945 and 1968, the GOP generally turned to midwestern conservatives for congressional leadership. The Senate especially witnessed this phenomenon as Vandenberg, Taft, and Dirksen all took their turn as foreign policy spokesmen for their party. During the 1960s Halleck and Ford led the House; Ford was much more open to new ideas and realized that the Republican party had to move forward and gain credibility if it were ever to win control of American government. As one reflects upon the Republican leaders during the 1960s, the styles of leadership varied dramatically. Halleck and Dirksen became passé by 1964. Dirksen was able to retain his Senate position because he never suffered the loss of Republican seats as Halleck had during 1964. Ford, on the other hand, was more incisive with his commentary and allowed for dynamic change. Dirksen was virtually encased in his leadership role as the loyal supporter of Lyndon Johnson. Ford represented a younger, more innovative group of Republican politicians, while Dirksen maintained the status quo and aided Johnson politically by moving to stem the tide of Republican criticism on war policy during the 1960s. Several others, such as Melvin Laird and Charles Goodell, also were instrumental. Laird, as chairman of the House conference, endorsed the changes, worked with Ford, and in some cases offered his own stinging critiques of Johnson's Vietnam policy. Goodell served as chairman of planning and research which sought clarification and intelligent criticism of administration policies.

The importance of these individuals cannot be overstated. They may not have drastically altered war policy—and it is doubtful if they did—but Lyndon Johnson knew of their existence within the political process. What ranks with greater certainty, however, was the fact that some Republicans were moving in new directions with positive changes. The irony, of course, is that Dirksen would not allow for these innovations within the Senate. Most assuredly, the Senate was—and is—different; it is a unique part of the national government by virtue of its small size. Dirksen was reluctant to change, and it emanated from the need to control his national power base as minority leader. Part of it may have been his age, since the "young Turks" were moving in and he faced challenges in the Senate despite his flamboyance and political acumen.

Dirksen was a multifaceted individual, a man of many contrasts. His political skill was exceptional, and he sought to exercise his influence at critical points. A truly fascinating book by Neil MacNeil entitled *Dirksen: Portrait of a Public Man* illustrates the skill and, in some cases, the serious shortcomings of this special senator. MacNeil argues that Dirksen's power within the Senate and the nation grew stronger when Johnson became president. Senator Mike Mansfield of Montana had taken the majority leader's position in the early 1960s. This, combined with other factors, gave Dirksen the opportunity to further develop his style, use the rules of unlimited Senate debate, and threaten, or actually invoke, the filibuster. Consequently, he worked his will. Mansfield was even quoted as saying, "You get a partner like Dirksen and form a dream relationship once in a century."[1] The crucial relationship, though, was with Lyndon Johnson, and an excellent rapport existed between the president and the Republican minority leader. As MacNeil has noted:

They were more than friends. They were intimates and they shared a confidential political kinship that negated traditional partisanship. Because of that special relationship, Dirksen gave to Johnson his unflagging support through the long ordeal of the Vietnam War. In this Dirksen stood against some of the most influential senators of the President's political party and, with even more telling effect, against the stalwarts of his own Republican Party. Repeatedly Dirksen acted to blunt, and even to silence, criticism by Republican leaders of Johnson's policies in Vietnam. He used what talents he possessed to defend the President against all faultfinders.[2]

It is also interesting to note how Dirksen's contemporaries viewed him nearly two decades after his death. Bob Wilson, former congressman from California, has noted that the joint leadership, and Dirksen in particular, took the classic statesman's role, but he also believes Dirksen took the role of commander in chief too literally. He further argues that Dirksen was not oriented to foreign policy; rather his interests were primarily domestic in nature. Wilson contends that Gerald Ford may have been more influential since he was the ranking member on the Defense Appropriations Subcommittee which made him more knowledgeable about defense policy.[3]

Hugh Scott, a Senate contemporary (and in some circles viewed as a rival to Dirksen), claims Dirksen and LBJ were on the same path in terms of Vietnam. To use Scott's phrase, "the emotional factor was there."[4] According to Scott, Dirksen tried to keep party people in line. He usually would give a speech at the Senate Republican Policy Committee meeting based on the appeal that Republicans could not be in opposition to a war in which we were currently engaged.

Charles Goodell, former congressman and senator from New

York, also feels Dirksen was in synchronization with Johnson on war policy and that he needed to give support in order that the quid pro quo of politics could be maintained. Goodell explains the pragmatism this way: "I know he would work out with Lyndon Johnson what was possible to get through the United States Senate, and where they would get the votes, . . . and what Everett Dirksen did to get the votes."[5]

Gerald Ford has observed that Dirksen was less critical than most Republicans of Johnson's war policy. Ford succinctly stated the difference between himself and the Senate minority leader: "I strongly felt that although I agreed with the goals of the Johnson administration in Vietnam, I vigorously criticized their prosecution of the war. Now, Dirksen never took that same hard-line position that I took."[6]

Melvin Laird, former congressman from Wisconsin, has commented that he is uncertain if Dirksen and LBJ were too close. Rather, he has referred to Dirksen's reasoning on Vietnam. The logic went as follows: Dirksen believed Republicans had won the 1952 election because of their stand on Korea. Therefore, they could benefit indirectly, and maybe directly, in the political sense, during the 1968 elections if the proper position was adopted. All-out criticism would only hurt the Republican position. Dirksen felt they had to be on the fringes. Attention to the conflict would be brought by the public because it would tire of the commitment to the war. Any definite plans for solving the war put the minority party on the defensive. The GOP strategy, by 1968 at least, was to put the administration on the defensive. Laird, of course, disagreed with this stance, but his control went only as far as the House of Representatives.[7]

A continuous theme appears during the late 1960s, and it was a question of some importance. Was the minority party fulfilling its traditional role as the loyal opposition? The answer is truly difficult to ascertain. It is clear that, after 1965, the House, under Ford's leadership, was moving to criticize Johnson and offer some constructive alternatives. Dirksen, however, preferred to side with the administration many times for personal and political reasons.

A more fundamental issue than leadership styles and personalities emerges from this time period. It was quite simply a matter of political subversion, not of the majority but a continuous tactic used against the minority. Research indicates that John F. Kennedy and especially Lyndon B. Johnson had several unique advantages over congressional Republicans. According to documents within the JFK Library in Boston, a conscious attempt was made to infiltrate the Republican decision-making process on Capitol Hill. Kennedy and Johnson maintained a Congressional Liaison Office on the Hill. Larry O'Brien oversaw this operation for JFK, and one of his people in the Liaison Office was Mike Manatos who handled Senate contacts on behalf of the White House.

In a memo dated February 15, 1961, Manatos told O'Brien that a man named Art Burgess was willing "to cooperate in the enactment of 'worthwhile' legislation." Manatos had known Burgess for years and described Burgess as a former newspaperman, a partisan Republican, and "absolutely trustworthy." Burgess's position as a staff member on the Senate Republican Policy Committee gave him access to confidential dealings of the minority, and he also knew how individual Senators would vote concerning key issues.[8] This "leak," cultivated during Kennedy's administration, had his role expanded during Johnson's tenure as president. Through the years, Burgess proved to be a valuable source of information. In numerous memos to Johnson, Manatos was able to outline Republican plans and thinking. For instance, Manatos quoted a tentative statement made during a noon meeting of the policy committee on March 8, 1966, which dealt with budgetary concerns.[9] The memo bears a time of 2:30 P.M., so within a matter of several hours, Manatos secured the information and forwarded it to the White House.

There are other references to this source through the years that Johnson was president. For example, Republican feelings on certain nominees for the Supreme Court during 1968 were transmitted to the White House. Burgess also gave detailed comments on a policy committee meeting during July 1968 where Republican strategy over these nominations was discussed.[10] In some cases Manatos therefore was able to confirm through Burgess what Dirksen was telling the administration. Granted, all of these matters were domestic issues, but several other documents bring into question not only Dirksen's role behind the scenes but other Republicans as well.

Jack Valenti, another key Johnson aide, reported in a memo to the president on February 2, 1966, that Dirksen told him he made a speech and had quoted "pertinent points to General Eisenhower's statement supporting the President's decision in Vietnam. Senator Dirksen wanted me to know that the 'mission was accomplished.' "[11] On June 29, 1966, White House aide Marvin Watson reported to LBJ the following: "Senator Dirksen called and said he made a favorable statement supporting the bombing of North Vietnam. The Senator said the purpose was to offset things that had been said by our Senator friends from Oregon and New York."[12]

Collaboration also can be seen with Senator Thomas Kuchel, Dirksen's whip in the Senate. Kuchel, in late 1966, wanted to make a speech favorable to deployment of antiballistic missiles and wanted White House commentary about and guidance for his efforts. Aides were scrambling behind the scenes in order to prepare a response because, as one aide wrote to Walt Rostow, Johnson's second national security advisor, "I understand that other Republicans are prepared to follow the lead taken by Kuchel. A sympathetic response—it need not accept his suggestions per se—would help him counterbalance Nixon in Republican circles."[13] A year later, on October 2, 1967, another memo reached the White House from Irvin Sprague to Marvin Watson. The subject was Kuchel and Vietnam.

I just talked to Ewing Haas (Kuchel's AA) [administrative assistant] in Los Angeles and he said Tom Kuchel is preparing a speech on Vietnam in which he takes the position that you can't stop the bombing unless you get some assurance from the other side. He said Tom will have some static about target selection, but in the main his position will be supportive of the President. Kuchel has just returned from Vietnam.[14]

An unusual sidelight to this relationship between Kuchel and Johnson can be seen from early in 1967. One aide reported Kuchel was just "a little envious" because a lot of people around him had gold presidential cuff links. Johnson directed he was to receive a pair with the compliments of the president.[15]

By 1968 the war was a political—not a military—disaster. In a memo to Johnson dated March 27, 1968, White House aide Charles Roche notified the president about political ramifications over Vietnam and problems within the Democratic party. The night before, Roche had spoken with Kenneth O'Donnell, who had been a top aide to JFK in the early 1960s. Their conversation was summarized to illustrate how Democrats were divided over issues of war and peace. The last part of the memo, though, revealed the desperate position in which the administration found itself. Roche then suggested using an article from Eisenhower, which had appeared in the *Readers' Digest* recently, because it would be

favorable to the Administration's position when compared to [Senator Robert] Kennedy and [Senator Eugene] McCarthy. I talked to Marvin Watson about the possibility of extracting from it and exploiting it in spots for the Wisconsin campaign. I do think, however, that it is important to concentrate criticism, even when Eisenhower uses the vehicle, on the weirdos and beatniks—not the regular people who have reservations about Vietnam.[16]

By the summer of 1968, the presidential campaign was taking shape. On August 15, Manatos sent Johnson a memo which synthesized conversation from a meeting with Dirksen. Two paragraphs are especially fascinating:

Dirksen was in an expansive mood when I saw him. He indicates that television seems to be killing the convention process, and that despite all of the carefully laid plans, he was unable to hear speeches from the floor when he sat as a member of the Illinois delegation. He seemed mighty pleased about his own performance, which I told him was excellent.

On the question of Governor Spiro Agnew as the Vice-Presidential nominee, I got the impression that Strom Thurmond's prominence is hurting the Republican party considerably. Dirksen went to great lengths to explain to me that when he and Jerry Ford and others saw Nixon on the morning after Nixon's nomination, there was never a word uttered about Agnew. Dirksen told me that he and others succeeded in knocking out some of the prospective Vice-Presidential nominees. He said, for instance, that he explained to Nixon that if John Lindsay were the number two man, it would take him about two weeks to assume the mantle of the chief candidate, and that in Dirksen's view, Lindsay's selection would be a mistake.[17]

These memoranda illustrate the nature of American politics, the exchanging of ideas, and the compromising within a democracy. The irony in all these situations is that Republicans basically supported LBJ on the Vietnam War. Johnson, however, was equally concerned about his domestic programs and sought to control that situation through a form of political subversion. In the domestic sense, the source of Senate sentiment provided useful information concerning Republican challenges, their mood, and their strategy. This breach of internal Republican organizational security provided an even further complication for the party out of power. If a staff member has been placed in a position of trust, why violate it? As part of the traditional patronage structure, Burgess had a position of trust, and if he disagreed with GOP philosophy, why use this method to bring about a change? A further problem was the payment for this information. What sort of reward came from this function? It also would seem that if one faced a serious matter of conscience, some other action would be in order rather than subversion which clearly helped undermine the Republican position on Capitol Hill.

From the foreign policy angle, and especially with Vietnam, LBJ relied upon his personal persuasive powers to cajole the minority into an acceptance or a bland acquiescence of his position. If this proved unsuccessful, Dirksen moved to ease the administration's burden. Dirksen, just as persuasive as Johnson but with less patronage power, could summon fellow Republicans to the cause, or at least stifle the dissent. Johnson also sought to blunt the critical impact of House Republicans, but he was less successful there since he lacked a spokesman like Dirksen. It now appears LBJ had little impact upon individuals such as Nixon who, as party leader, attempted to chart a GOP plan of alternatives for whatever political, philosophical, or personal reasons.

The question then arises, if Dirksen had allowed for innovations as Ford did and had not been so closely aligned with Johnson, could Republicans have made a difference in the outcome of the Vietnam War? Republican options were limited due to their philosophical approach of keeping Vietnam free but they may have argued more forcefully for a different strategy in the fighting. Dirksen, with his stature as a national leader, could have exerted influence to bring such a situation into the forefront of administration thinking. In tandem with Gerald Ford, Dirksen might have accomplished a great deal to change Johnson's incremental strategy. This does not belie the fact, however, that there are two areas of thought in this post-Vietnam period on conduct of the war. One side argues that military tactics were inappropriately applied, that military power was wasted, and that incrementalism as a policy was incorrect. The other group argues that no matter what we did in Vietnam, the war never would have been won because the population and terrain would not support a prolonged conflict no matter how much military power was engaged. No war is purely military strategy. Politics always enters the scene, because ultimately the politicians determine war policy.

What is of concern, though, is the philosophical role of the opposition party during a non-declared war. Vandenberg called for unity on America's role overseas, but he did theorize that dissent was to stop at the water's edge; free and active constructive criticism was, and should be, an essential mark of American democracy. During the mid- and late 1960s, Republicans in the House evaluated Johnson's policies on Vietnam. On the other hand, Republican senators were more cautious, but their direct access to the administration, and Dirksen's presence, blunted even these cautious voices.

Gerald Ford performed his role as minority leader in an admirable way. As a man of integrity and good will, he sought to question Lyndon Johnson's policies, point out contradictions, and generally follow the spirit of bipartisanship. Dirksen, on the other hand, represented a paradox. The Senate minority leader gladly went to the forefront of Republican leaders, took to the limelight, and offered his own brand of criticism. As a master of political skills, he waited for a propitious occasion to criticize Johnson deftly. In most cases, his attacks upon LBJ were minimal, and he never allowed opposition policy to be formulated as Ford had done. Therein lies the contradiction, or difference in philosophy, between these two congressional leaders. Whether this situation stemmed from practical political necessity or sheer vanity on Dirksen's part may never be known.

Beyond Ford and Dirksen, the underlying problem was that the Vietnam War put an unusual strain upon bipartisanship. The length of the war, its limited nature through containment and Johnson's policy, and the eventual public dissent paralyzed the nation and its leaders. Another very crucial problem was the fact that the public was misled about America's goal to win in Vietnam. Dirksen, either directly or indirectly, helped perpetuate this myth. Consequently, an inevitable cynicism grew out of this period, a feeling that still affects our politics and the people's relationship to their government.

The increasing need for continuity in our foreign policy is self-evident as each year passes. The national interest demands that America's leaders operate from a position of mutual understanding, that national goals be clearly stated, clarified, and re-evaluated when necessary. Political opposition within our government is important because the nation benefits from vigorous dissent. This vigorous, constructive questioning can open the door for fresh ideas and allow for compromises to be made; that is the essential strength of American democracy and the conduct of foreign affairs.

British statesman Lord Boyd Orr once remarked that communism was not necessarily a Kremlin strategy but rather "hunger made articulate."[18] Perhaps America lost sight of that fact since World War II. The real threat to our national interest may lie in a mistaken perception of the world and not viewing situations clearly and precisely. Without the open debate and clarification of issues, we are relegated to repeating similar errors as we move through the balance of this century and into the next one.

It is important to re-evaluate the meaning and position for the loyal opposition in our governmental structure. Vandenberg's thesis is still viable if we follow his suggestion of a cogent examination of the issues at hand. Vietnam did not forever mute the effectiveness of the minority political party, nor did it forever strangle the power of the United States. As a matter of practicality, foreign policy discussions should occur between the president and Congress, but the lead will usually rest with the president. The last forty years have made this fact exceedingly clear. However, the Congress needs to perform its role by helping develop a clear consensus on the national interest. Competent, intelligent, well-educated, and committed leaders in Congress and the presidency can enhance America's role as a world power. Moving the United States towards the envisioned goals will, in the long term, strengthen America and the rest of the free world.

NOTES

1. THE MANTLE OF WORLD LEADERSHIP

1. George Mayer, *The Republican Party 1854–1964* (New York: Oxford University Press, 1964), p. 450.

2. Hans J. Morgenthau, "The Founding Fathers and Foreign Policy," *Orbis* (Spring 1976), p. 18.

3. Interview with Senator Hugh Scott and the author, Washington, D.C., September 1982.

4. Thomas A. Bailey, *Democrats v. Republicans. The Continuing Clash* (New York: Meredith Press, 1968), p. 147.

5. John Spanier, *American Foreign Policy Since World War II*, 9th ed. (New York: Holt, Rinehart and Winston, 1983), pp. 4–20.

6. Norman Graebner, *Cold War Diplomacy: American Foreign Policy, 1945–1960* (Princeton, N.J.: D. Van Nostrand Company, 1962), p. 27.

7. Interview with Senator John Tower and the author, Washington, D.C., July 1983.

8. A. H. Vandenberg, Jr., ed., *The Private Papers of Senator Vandenberg* (Boston: Houghton Mifflin Company, 1952), p. 1.

9. *Congressional Record*, 18 March 1947, p. 2167.

10. Vandenberg, *Private Papers*, p. 450.

11. Ibid., p. 550.

12. Malcolm E. Jewell, *Senatorial Politics and Foreign Policy* (Lexington: University of Kentucky Press, 1962), p. 209.

13. Ibid., pp. 37–39.

14. Holbert N. Carroll, *The House of Representatives and Foreign Policy* (Boston: Little, Brown and Company, 1966), pp. 270–71.

15. Ronald Caridi, "The GOP and the Korean War," *Pacific Quarterly Review* (November 1968), pp. 422–26.

16. Robert A. Taft, *A Foreign Policy for Americans* (Garden City, N.Y.: Doubleday and Company, 1951), p. 112.

17. Ibid., pp. 11–12.

18. James T. Patterson, *Mr. Republican: A Biography of Robert A. Taft* (Boston: Houghton Mifflin Company, 1976), p. 454.

19. Jewell, *Senatorial Politics and Foreign Policy*, p. 73.

20. Spanier, *American Foreign Policy*, p. 69.

21. John Spanier, *The Truman-MacArthur Controversy and the Korean War* (New York: W. W. Norton and Company, 1965), pp. 151–54.

22. Ibid., p. 269.

23. Thomas A. Bailey, *A Diplomatic History of the American People*, 9th ed. (Englewood Cliffs, N.J.: Prentice-Hall, 1974), pp. 824–25.

24. Ibid., p. 824.

25. Caridi, "The GOP and the Korean War," p. 436.

26. Ibid., p. 439.

27. Russell Fifield, *Southeast Asia in United States Policy*, 4th printing (New York: Frederick Praeger, 1967), pp. 33–35.

28. Graebner, *Cold War Diplomacy*, p. 35.

29. Dwight D. Eisenhower, *Mandate for Change, 1953–1956* (Garden City, N.Y.: Doubleday and Company, 1963), p. 338.

30. Spanier, *American Foreign Policy*, p. 77.

31. Robert A. Divine, *Eisenhower and the Cold War* (New York: Oxford University Press, 1981), pp. 33–38.

32. Ibid., pp. 39–44.

33. Stephen E. Ambrose, *Eisenhower* (New York: Simon and Schuster, 1984), p. 173.

34. Ibid., p. 177.

35. Peter Poole, *The United States and Indochina, from FDR to Nixon* (Hinsdale, Ill.: Dryden Press, 1973), pp. 31–36.

36. Ibid., p. 47.

37. Graebner, *Cold War Diplomacy*, p. 94.

38. Eisenhower, *Mandate for Change*, p. 373.

39. Jewell, *Senatorial Politics and Foreign Policy*, pp. 91–92.

40. Carroll, *The House and Foreign Policy*, pp. 268–69.

41. Jewell, *Senatorial Politics and Foreign Policy*, p. 96.

42. Ibid., p. 43.

43. Interview with Mr. Charles A. Halleck and the author, Rensselaer, Ind., November 1979.

44. *New York Times*, 30 September 1960.

45. Theodore H. White, *The Making of the President 1960* (New York: Atheneum House, 1961), pp. 192–93.

46. Ibid., p. 191.

47. Republican National Committee, *Official Report of the Twenty-seventh Republican National Convention* (Chicago, Ill., July 25–28, 1960), p. 235.

48. U.S. Congress, Senate, *Republican Review of the First Session*, S. Doc. 60, 86th Cong., 1st sess., 1959, p. 53.

2. THE EV AND CHARLIE SHOW VS. JFK

1. Roger Hilsman, *To Move a Nation* (New York: Dell Publishing Company, 1967), p. 19.
2. Ibid., p. 53.
3. Theodore C. Sorenson, *Kennedy* (New York: Harper and Row, 1965), p. 509.
4. Ibid., p. 350.
5. U.S. Congress, Senate, *A Record of Press Conference Statements for the Joint Senate-House Republican Leadership*, S. Doc. 63, 87th Cong., 1st sess., 1961, p. iii.
6. Henry Z. Scheele, *Charlie Halleck: A Political Biography* (New York: Exposition Press, 1966), p. 207.
7. Ibid., pp. 206–8.
8. U.S. Congress, Senate, *Achievements During Eight Years of a Republican Administration*, S. Doc. 23, 87th Cong., 1st sess., 1961, p. 6.
9. *Press Statement for Republican Leadership*, 87th Cong., 1st sess., p. 6.
10. Ibid., p. 7.
11. Kenneth Crawford, "The Loyal Opposition," *Newsweek*, September 18, 1961, p. 35.
12. Sorenson, *Kennedy*, p. 510.
13. Herbert Parmet, *JFK* (New York: Dial Press, 1983), p. 195.
14. *Press Statements for Republican Leadership*, 87th Cong., 1st sess., p. 4.
15. Ibid., pp. 7–8.
16. Parmet, *JFK*, p. 177.
17. Ibid., pp. 176–77.
18. *New York Times*, 23 April 1961.
19. *New York Times*, 21 April 1961.
20. *New York Times*, 22 April 1961.
21. *New York Times*, 26 April 1961.
22. *New York Times*, 21 April 1961.
23. *New York Times*, 28 April 1961.
24. Ibid.
25. *New York Times*, 3 May 1961.
26. *New York Times*, 10 May 1961.
27. *New York Times*, 25 May 1961.
28. *New York Times*, 28 May 1961.
29. *New York Times*, 15 July 1961.
30. *New York Times*, 9 February 1962.

31. *New York Times*, 20 February 1962.
32. *New York Times*, 26 March 1962.
33. *New York Times*, 8 June 1962.
34. *New York Times*, 30 June 1962.
35. U.S. Congress, Senate, *A Record of Press Conference Statements for the Joint Senate-House Leadership*, S. Doc. 158, 87th Cong., 2nd sess., pp. 11–12.
36. Ibid., p. 15.
37. Montague Kern, Patricia Levering, and Ralph Levering, *The Kennedy Crises* (Chapel Hill: The University of North Carolina Press, 1983), pp. 99–100.
38. *New York Times*, 5 September 1962.
39. Ibid.
40. *New York Times*, 15 September 1962.
41. *New York Times*, 19 September 1962.
42. Kern and Levering, *The Kennedy Crises*, p. 120.
43. Ibid., p. 108.
44. Ibid., p. 100.
45. *New York Times*, 23 October 1962.
46. Ibid.
47. *New York Times*, 24 October 1962.
48. Ibid.
49. *New York Times*, 7 October 1962.
50. *New York Times*, 29 October 1962.
51. Congressional Quarterly Service, *Congress and the Nation 1954–1964* (Washington, D.C.: Congressional Quarterly Service, 1965), pp. 45–46.
52. U.S. Congress, Senate, *A Record of Press Conference Statements for the Joint Senate-House Republican Leadership*. S. Doc. 52, 88th Cong., 1st sess., p. 15.
53. Ibid., p. 23.
54. *New York Times*, 13 November 1962.
55. *New York Times*, 14 February 1963.
56. *New York Times*, 19 February 1963.
57. *New York Times*, 9 March 1963.
58. Arthur M. Schlesinger, Jr., *A Thousand Days* (Boston: Houghton Mifflin Company, 1965), p. 321.
59. Parmet, *JFK*, p. 133.
60. *Press Statements for Republican Leadership*, 87th Cong., 2nd sess, p. 9.
61. Ibid., p. 13.
62. Parmet, *JFK*, p. 326.
63. Frances FitzGerald, *Fire in the Lake. The Vietnamese and the Americans in Vietnam* (New York: Vintage Books, 1973), p. 138.

64. Hilsman, *Move a Nation*, pp. 413–14.

65. John F. Kennedy, *The Strategy of Peace*, edited by Allan Nevins (New York: Harper and Brothers, 1960), p. 57.

66. Leslie Gelb and Richard Betts, *The Irony of Vietnam: The System Worked* (Washington, D.C.: Brookings Institution, 1979), p. 80.

67. Parmet, *JFK*, pp. 334–35.

68. *New York Times*, 11 April 1963.

69. Kern and Levering, *Kennedy Crises*, p. 176.

70. Parmet, *JFK*, pp. 331–36.

71. *New York Times*, 25 October 1963.

3. THE GRAND OLD PARTY DIVIDED

1. Theodore H. White, *The Making of the President 1964* (New York: Atheneum Publishers, 1965), p. 43.

2. Eric F. Goldman, *The Tragedy of Lyndon Johnson* (New York: Alfred A. Knopf, 1969), p. 20.

3. Ibid., p. 25.

4. Leslie Gelb and Richard Betts, *The Irony of Vietnam: The System Worked* (Washington, D.C.: Brookings Institution, 1979), pp. 96–97.

5. U.S. Congress, Senate, *A Record of Press Conference Statements for the Joint Senate-House Republican Leadership*, S. Doc. 107, 88th Cong., 2nd sess., 1964, p. 8.

6. Everett Dirksen, NBC interview, "Meet the Press," 2 February 1964, mimeographed transcript from Remarks and Releases, 1941–1969, The Dirksen Center, Pekin, Ill.

7. *New York Times*, 28 February 1964.

8. *New York Times*, 22 April 1964.

9. Ibid.

10. *Press Statements for Republican Leadership*, 88th Cong., 2nd sess., p. 25.

11. *New York Times*, 30 January 1964.

12. *New York Times*, 23 February 1964.

13. *New York Times*, 19 April 1964.

14. *New York Times*, 3 May 1964.

15. *New York Times*, 1 June 1964.

16. White, *President 1964*, p. 62.

17. Ibid., pp. 73–83.

18. Joseph Persico, *The Imperial Rockefeller* (New York: Simon and Schuster, 1982), p. 80.

19. White, *President 1964*, pp. 210–13.

20. Ibid., p. 89.

21. Barry Goldwater, *Where I Stand* (New York: McGraw-Hill, 1964), p. 28.

22. *New York Times*, 19 March 1964.

23. *New York Times*, 12 May 1964.

24. *New York Times*, 25 May 1964.

25. *New York Times*, 10 July 1964.

26. Persico, *The Imperial Rockefeller*, p. 72.

27. Ibid., p. 85.

28. *New York Times*, 30 January 1964.

29. *New York Times*, 24 February 1964.

30. *New York Times*, 28 April 1964.

31. *New York Times*, 20 May 1964.

32. Republican National Committee, *Official Report of the Proceedings of the Twenty-eighth Republican National Convention* (San Francisco, Calif., July 13–16, 1964), p. 266.

33. Ibid., p. 267.

34. Ibid., pp. 414 and 416.

35. White, *President 1964*, p. 220.

36. *New York Times*, 3 August 1964.

37. "The 'Phantom Battle' That Led To War," *U.S. News*, July 23, 1984, pp. 56–64.

38. Walter A. Zelman, *Senate Dissent and the Vietnam War, 1964–1968* (Ann Arbor, Mich.: University Microfilms, 1971), p. 237.

39. Gelb and Betts, *The Irony of Vietnam*, p. 103.

40. Zelman, *Senate Dissent and Vietnam*, pp. 81–82.

41. Ibid., p. 84.

42. Gelb and Betts, *The Irony of Vietnam*, p. 108.

43. Ibid., p. 118.

44. *New York Times*, 5 August 1964.

45. *New York Times*, 23 April 1964.

46. *New York Times*, 23 September 1964.

47. *New York Times*, 24 September 1964.

48. *New York Times*, 30 September 1964.

49. *New York Times*, 1 October 1964.

50. *New York Times*, 21 October 1964.

51. *New York Times*, 6 October 1964.

52. *New York Times*, 21 October 1964.

53. Ibid.

54. Ibid.

55. *New York Times*, 2 November 1964.

56. *New York Times*, 3 November 1964.

57. Henry Z. Scheele, *Charlie Halleck: A Political Biography* (New York: Exposition Press, 1966), p. 243.

58. Robert L. Peabody, "Political Parties: House Republican Leadership," in *American Political Institutions and Public Policy*, edited by Allan P. Sindler (Boston: Little, Brown and Company, 1969), pp. 185–86.

59. Ibid.

60. Scheele, *Charlie Halleck*, p. 253.

61. Interview with Mr. Bob Wilson and the author, Washington, D.C., September 1982.

62. Interview with Senator Charles Goodell and the author, Washington, D.C., June 1983.

63. Ibid.

64. Ibid.

65. Interview with President Gerald Ford and the author, Rancho Mirage, Calif., December 1982.

66. Interview with Mr. Melvin Laird and the author, Washington, D.C., July 1983.

67. Goodell interview, June 1983.

68. Ibid.

69. Ford interview, December 1982.

70. Ibid.

71. Laird interview, July 1983.

72. Ford interview, December 1982.

73. Laird interview, July 1983.

74. Interview with Dr. William Prendergast and the author, Washington, D.C., June 1983.

75. Ibid.

76. Ibid.

77. Ford interview, December 1982.

78. Prendergast interview, June 1983.

79. Laird interview, July 1983.

80. Goodell interview, June 1983.

81. Laird interview, July 1983.

82. Goodell interview, June 1983.

83. Prendergast interview, June 1983.

84. Ibid.

85. Goodell interview, June 1983.

86. Prendergast interview, June 1983.

87. Ibid.

88. Interview with Governor George Romney and the author, Bloomfield Hills, Mich., July 1984.

89. Ford interview, December 1982.

90. Laird interview, July 1983.

91. Romney interview, July 1984.

92. U.S. Congress, Senate, *A Record of Press Conference Statements for*

the Joint Senate-House Republican Leadership, Doc. 68, 89th Cong., 1st sess., 1965, p. 15.

93. Ibid., p. 16.

94. Dirksen Papers, "Tentative Agenda for the First Meeting of the Republican Coordinating Committee," mimeographed sheet from Republican Congressional Leadership Papers, f. 55, The Dirksen Center, Pekin, Ill.

95. Wilson interview, September 1982.

96. *New York Times*, 11 March 1965.

97. Romney interview, July 1984.

98. Prendergast interview, June 1983.

99. Republican Coordinating Committee, *Choice for America, Reports of the Republican Coordinating Committee*, Washington, D.C., "United States Foreign Policy in Vietnam," June 1965, p. 324.

100. Ibid., p. 325.

101. *New York Times*, 7 May 1965.

102. Richard M. Nixon, *RN: The Memoirs of Richard Nixon* (New York: Grosset and Dunlop, 1978), p. 264.

103. Interview with Senator John Tower and the author, Washington, D.C., July 1983.

104. Ford interview, December 1982.

105. Laird interview, July 1983.

106. *New York Times*, 3 January 1965.

107. Everett Dirksen, NBC interview, "Meet the Press," 24 January 1965, mimeographed transcript from Remarks and Releases, 1941–1969, The Dirksen Center, Pekin, Ill.

108. Prendergast interview, June 1983.

109. *New York Times*, 27 January 1965.

110. Zelman, *Senate Dissent and Vietnam*, p. 128.

111. *New York Times*, 11 February 1965.

112. *New York Times*, 25 April 1965.

113. Stephen E. Ambrose, *Eisenhower* (New York: Simon and Schuster, 1984), p. 656.

114. Ibid., p. 657.

115. Ibid., p. 658.

116. Ibid., p. 661.

117. *New York Times*, 14 May 1965.

118. *New York Times*, 17 June 1965.

119. Everett Dirksen, "A Capsule Story of Vietnam," T.V. and Radio Weekly Report, 21 June 1965, mimeographed transcript from Remarks and Releases, 1941–1969, The Dirksen Center, Pekin, Ill.

120. Romney interview, July 1984.

121. *New York Times*, 27 July 1985.

122. *New York Times*, 22 July 1965.

123. *New York Times*, 17 June 1965.

124. *New York Times*, 25 June 1965.

125. *New York Times*, 11 July 1965.

126. Gelb and Betts, *The Irony of Vietnam*, p. 132.

127. Ibid., p. 137.

128. Ibid., p. 158.

129. Everett Dirksen, CBS interview, "Face the Nation," 19 September 1965, mimeographed transcript from Remarks and Releases, 1941–1969, The Dirksen Center, Pekin, Ill.

130. *New York Times*, 19 October 1965.

131. *New York Times*, 3 November 1965.

4. THE OIL CAN AND THE SWORD

1. Republican Coordinating Committee, *Choice for America*, Republican National Committee, Washington, D.C., 1968, "Vietnam," p. 475.

2. *New York Times*, 8 January 1966.

3. Everett Dirksen, ABC interview, "Issues and Answers," 9 January 1966, mimeographed transcript from Remarks and Releases, 1941–1969, The Dirksen Center, Pekin, Ill.

4. Ibid.

5. Everett Dirksen, NBC interview, "The Today Show," 11 January 1966, mimeographed transcript from Remarks and Releases, 1941–1969, The Dirksen Center, Pekin, Ill.

6. Ibid.

7. U.S. President, *Public Papers of the Presidents of the United States* (Washington, D.C.: Office of the *Federal Register*, National Archives and Records Service, 1963–69), Lyndon B. Johnson, 1966, pp. 7 and 10.

8. Interview with Dr. William Prendergast and the author, Washington, D.C., June 1983.

9. *New York Times*, 18 January 1966.

10. Interview with President Gerald Ford and the author, Rancho Mirage, Calif., December 1982.

11. *New York Times*, 19 January 1966.

12. *New York Times*, 15 January 1966.

13. *New York Times*, 30 January 1966.

14. *New York Times*, 31 January 1966.

15. *New York Times*, 13 February 1966.

16. *New York Times*, 13 March 1966.

17. Interview with Senator J. William Fulbright and the author, Washington, D.C., November 1981.

18. *New York Times*, 25 February 1966.

19. *New York Times*, 3 March 1966.
20. *New York Times*, 1 May 1966.
21. Everett Dirksen, "The Commander and Chief," T.V. and Radio Weekly Report, 21 February 1966, mimeographed transcript from Remarks and Releases, 1941–1969, The Dirksen Center, Pekin, Ill.
22. *New York Times*, 3 March 1966.
23. Interview with Mr. Bob Wilson and the author, Washington, D.C., September 1982.
24. *New York Times*, 1 May 1966.
25. *New York Times*, 18 March 1966.
26. Ford interview, December 1982.
27. *New York Times*, 19 April 1966.
28. *New York Times*, 20 April 1966.
29. Ibid.
30. *New York Times*, 21 April 1966.
31. *New York Times*, 22 April 1966.
32. Ford interview, December 1982.
33. Ibid.
34. Prendergast interview, June 1983.
35. Ford interview, December 1982.
36. *New York Times*, 25 May 1966.
37. *New York Times*, 10 June 1966.
38. *New York Times*, 12 June 1966.
39. Ibid.
40. *New York Times*, 20 June 1966.
41. *New York Times*, 30 June 1966.
42. *New York Times*, 13 June 1966.
43. *New York Times*, 5 July 1966.
44. *New York Times*, 6 August 1966.
45. *New York Times*, 8 August 1966.
46. Eric F. Goldman, *The Tragedy of Lyndon Johnson* (New York: Alfred A. Knopf, 1969), pp. 498–502.
47. *New York Times*, 6 June 1966.
48. *New York Times*, 24 August 1966.
49. *New York Times*, 27 August 1966.
50. *New York Times*, 26 August 1966.
51. *New York Times*, 28 September 1966.
52. Republican Coordinating Committee, *Choice for America*, "Vietnam and the Manila Conference," p. 481.
53. *New York Times*, 1 September 1966.
54. *New York Times*, 17 September 1966.
55. *New York Times*, 12 September 1966.
56. *New York Times*, 14 September 1966.

57. Joint Senate-House Republican Leadership Minutes, One hundred and thirty-second meeting, 21 September 1966, mimeographed transcript from Republican Congressional Leadership Papers, f. 71, The Dirksen Center, Pekin, Ill.

58. Republican Conference of the House of Representatives, *The United States and the War in Vietnam* (Washington, D.C.), 20 September 1966, p. 2.

59. Ibid., p. 31.

60. U.S. Congress, Senate, *A Record of Press Conference Statements for the Republican Leadership of of the Congress*, S. Doc. 118, 89th Cong., 2nd sess., 1966, p. 31.

61. *New York Times*, 14 October 1966.

62. *New York Times*, 15 October 1966.

63. *New York Times*, 1 November 1966.

64. *New York Times*, 3 November 1966.

65. Interview with Mr. William Baroody and the author, Washington, D.C., September 1984.

66. Ibid.

67. *New York Times*, 20 January 1967.

68. U.S. Congress, Senate, *Where Our Nation Stands at Home and Abroad*, S. Doc. 116, 89th Cong., 2nd sess., 1966, pp. 1, 2, and 13.

69. *New York Times*, 3 February 1967.

70. *New York Times*, 24 March 1967.

71. *New York Times*, 4 March 1967.

72. *New York Times*, 27 March 1967.

73. *New York Times*, 12 February 1967.

74. *New York Times*, 19 February 1967.

75. *New York Times*, 22 February 1967.

76. *New York Times*, 8 April 1967.

77. *New York Times*, 2 March 1967.

78. *New York Times*, 19 March 1967.

79. *New York Times*, 15 April 1967.

80. *New York Times*, 18 April 1967.

81. *New York Times*, 25 April 1967.

82. Walter A. Zelman, *Senate Dissent and the Vietnam War, 1964–1968*, (Ann Arbor, Mich.: University Microfilms, 1971) p. 163.

83. Senate Republican Policy Committee, "The War in Vietnam," April 1967, Washington, D.C., p. 91.

84. Ibid., p. 90.

85. Zelman, *Senate Dissent and Vietnam*, p. 287.

86. Ibid., p. 289.

87. *New York Times*, 3 May 1967.

88. *New York Times*, 8 May 1967.

89. Interview with Mr. Melvin Laird and the author, Washington, D.C., July 1983.

90. *New York Times*, 3 May 1967.

91. Ibid.

92. *New York Times*, 4 May 1967.

93. Ibid.

94. *New York Times*, 10 May 1967.

95. *New York Times*, 17 August 1967.

96. *New York Times*, 11 August 1967.

97. *New York Times*, 11 July 1967.

98. *New York Times*, 12 July 1967.

99. *New York Times*, 17 August 1967.

100. *New York Times*, 5 September 1967.

101. Everett Dirksen, CBS interview, "Face the Nation," 6 August 1967, mimeographed transcript from Remarks and Releases, 1941–1969, The Dirksen Center, Pekin, Ill.

102. Zelman, *Senate Dissent and Vietnam*, p. 272.

103. Ibid.

104. *New York Times*, 4 October 1967.

105. Ibid.

106. Ibid.

107. *New York Times*, 21 November 1967.

108. Zelman, *Senate Dissent and Vietnam*, p. 98.

109. Ibid., p. 184.

110. U.S. Congress, Senate, *A Record of Press Conference Statements for the Republican Leadership of the Congress*, S. Doc. 61, 90th Cong., 1st sess., 1967, p. 18.

111. Ibid., pp. 24–27.

112. U.S. Congress, Senate, *The Republican Report*, " 'Quo Vadis?' Whither America?" S. Doc. 62, 90th Cong., 1st sess., 1967, p. 2.

113. *New York Times*, 28 October 1967.

114. Interview with Governor George Romney and the author, Bloomfield Hills, Mich., July 1984.

115. *New York Times*, 8 December 1967.

116. Ibid.

117. Ibid.

118. *New York Times*, 29 November 1967.

119. *New York Times*, 30 November 1967.

120. *New York Times*, 25 December 1967.

121. *New York Times*, 15 January 1967.

122. Joint Senate-House Republican Leadership Minutes, One hundred and fifty-seventh meeting, 16 January 1968, mimeographed transcript from Republican Congressional Leadership Papers, f. 77, The Dirksen Center, Pekin, Ill.

123. Laird interview, July 1983.

124. Interview with Senator John Tower and the author, Washington, D.C., July 1983.

125. Ibid.

126. Robert L. Peabody, "Political Parties: House Republican Leadership," in *American Political Institutions and Public Policy*, edited by Allan P. Sindler (Boston: Little Brown and Company, 1969), p. 218.

127. Zelman, *Senate Dissent and Vietnam*, p. 330.

128. *New York Times*, 4 January 1968.

129. *New York Times*, 16 January 1968.

130. *New York Times*, 9 January 1968.

131. *New York Times*, 28 February 1968.

132. *New York Times*, 10 May 1968.

133. Theodore H. White, *The Making of the President 1968* (New York: Atheneum Publishers, 1969), pp. 230–38.

134. *New York Times*, 14 July 1968.

135. Richard M. Nixon, *RN: The Memoirs of Richard Nixon* (New York: Grosset and Dunlap, 1978), p. 279.

136. Stephen E. Ambrose, *Eisenhower* (New York: Simon and Schuster, 1984), p. 665.

137. *New York Times*, 6 February 1968.

138. *New York Times*, 14 February 1968.

139. *New York Times*, 6 March 1968.

140. *New York Times*, 11 March 1968.

141. *New York Times*, 21 March 1968.

142. *New York Times*, 4 May 1968.

143. *New York Times*, 18 April 1968.

144. Republican Coordinating Committee, *Choice for America*, "Democratic Foreign Policy: The Crisis of Confidence," p. 426.

145. Ibid.

146. Ibid.

147. Ford interview, December 1982.

148. *New York Times*, 2 August 1968.

149. Ibid.

150. *New York Times*, 29 July 1968.

151. *New York Times*, 1 August 1968.

152. *New York Times*, 2 August 1968.

153. Ibid.

154. Interview with Senator Charles Goodell and the author, Washington, D.C., June 1983.

155. Republican National Committee, *Official Report of the Proceedings of the Twenty-ninth Republican National Convention* (Miami Beach, Fla., August 5–8, 1968), pp. 263–64.

156. U.S. Congress, Senate, *A Record of Press Conference Statements for the Republican Leadership of the Congress*, S. Doc. 110, 90th Cong., 2nd sess., 1968, p. 13.

157. U.S. Congress, Senate, *The Republican Report*, "Dedication, Discipline, Duty," S. Doc. 113, 90th Cong., 2nd sess., 1968, p. 1.

158. *New York Times*, 8 October 1968.

159. *New York Times*, 18 October 1968.

160. *New York Times*, 1 November 1968.

5. A LEGACY OF TRANSITION

1. Neil MacNeil, *Dirksen: Portrait of a Public Man* (Cleveland, Ohio: World Publishing Company, 1970), p. 230.

2. Ibid., p. 272.

3. Interview with Mr. Bob Wilson and the author, Washington, D.C., September 1982.

4. Interview with Senator Hugh Scott and the author, Washington, D.C., September 1982.

5. Interview with Senator Charles Goodell and the author, Washington, D.C., June 1983.

6. Interview with President Gerald Ford and the author, Rancho Mirage, Calif., December 1982.

7. Interview with Mr. Melvin Laird and the author, Washington, D.C., July 1983.

8. Memo, Manatos to Lawrence O'Brien, February 15, 1961, filed in Box 1, Manatos Collection, JFK Library.

9. Memo, Manatos to the President, March 8, 1966, filed in the Everett Dirksen Name File, White House Central File, LBJ Library.

10. Memo, Manatos to the President, July 9, 1968, filed in the Everett Dirksen Name File, White House Central File, LBJ Library.

11. Memo, Valenti to the President, February 2, 1966, filed in the Everett Dirksen Name File, White House Central File, LBJ Library.

12. Memo, Watson to the President, June 29, 1966, filed in the Everett Dirksen Name File, White House Central File, LBJ Library.

13. Memo, Moose to Rostow, December 8, 1966, filed in the National Security File, File ND21, LBJ Library.

14. Memo, Sprague to Watson, October 2, 1967, filed in the Thomas Kuchel Name File, White House Central File, LBJ Library.

15. Memo, Watson to the President, March 23, 1967, filed in the Thomas Kuchel Name File, White House Central File, LBJ Library.

16. Memo, Roche to the President, March 27, 1968, filed in the Marvin Watson Files, Box 32, LBJ Library.

17. Memo, Manatos to the President, August 15, 1968, filed in the Everett Dirksen Name File, White House Central File, LBJ Library.

18. Esmond Wright, "Foreign Policy Since Dulles," *Political Quarterly* (April 1962), pp. 119–20.

BIBLIOGRAPHY

Ambrose, Stephen E. *Eisenhower*. New York: Simon and Schuster, 1984.

Angel, D. Duane. *Romney: A Political Biography*. New York: Exposition Press, 1967.

Austin, Anthony. *The President's War*. New York: J. B. Lippincott, 1971.

Bailey, Thomas A. *Democrats v. Republicans. The Continuing Clash*. New York: Meredith Press, 1968.

———. *A Diplomatic History of the American People*. 9th ed. Englewood Cliffs, N.J.: Prentice-Hall, 1974.

Baldwin, David A. "Congressional Initiative in Foreign Policy." *The Journal of Politics* (November 1966): 754–73.

Bax, Frans R. "The Legislative-Executive Relationship in Foreign Policy: New Partnership or New Competition?" *Orbis* (Winter 1977): 881–904.

Bennet, D. J. "Congress in Foreign Policy: Who Needs It?" *Foreign Affairs* (Fall 1978): 40–50.

Berger, Henry W. "Bipartisanship, Senator Taft, and the Truman Administration." *Political Science Quarterly* (Summer 1975): 221–37.

Bibby, John F. "The Goldwater Movement." *American Behavioral Scientist* (November 1973): 249–71.

Caridi, Ronald. "The GOP and the Korean War." *Pacific Historical Review* (November 1968): 423–43.

Carroll, Holbert N. *The House of Representatives and Foreign Affairs*. Boston: Little, Brown and Company, 1966.

Chester, Edward. *Sectionalism, Politics, and American Diplomacy*. Metuchen, N.J.: Scarecrow Press, Inc., 1975.

Crabb, Cecil. *Bipartisan Foreign Policy—Myth or Reality?* Evanston, Ill.: Row, Peterson and Company, 1957.

Crawford, Kenneth. "The Loyal Opposition." *Newsweek*, September 18, 1961, 35.

Dahl, Robert A. *Congress and Foreign Policy.* New York: Harcourt, Brace and Company, 1950.

Degler, Carl. "The Great Reversal: The Republican Party's First Century." *Southern Atlantic Quarterly* (Winter 1966): 1–11.

Divine, Robert A. *Eisenhower and the Cold War.* New York: Oxford University Press, 1981.

Eisenhower, Dwight D. *Mandate for Change, 1953–1956.* Garden City, N.Y.: Doubleday and Company, 1963.

Fifield, Russell. *Southeast Asia in United States Policy.* 4th printing. New York: Frederick Praeger, 1967.

FitzGerald, Frances. *Fire in the Lake. The Vietnamese and the Americans in Vietnam.* New York: Vintage Books, 1973.

Fitzsimmons, M. A. "Fifteen Years of American Foreign Policy." *The Review of Politics* (January 1961): 3–19.

Ford, Gerald R. *A Time to Heal: The Autobiography of Gerald Ford.* New York: Harper and Row, 1979.

Friedlander, Robert. "American Foreign Policy: Illusion and Reality." *Southern Atlantic Quarterly* (Autumn 1964): 468–77.

Fulbright, J. William. *The Arrogance of Power.* New York: Random House, 1966.

———. *Prospects for the West.* Cambridge, Mass.: Harvard University Press, 1963.

Gazell, James A. "Arthur H. Vandenberg, Internationalism, and the United Nations." *Political Science Quarterly* (September 1973): 375–94.

Gelb, Leslie, and Richard Betts. *The Irony of Vietnam: The System Worked.* Washington, D.C.: Brookings Institution, 1979.

Gerberding, William. "Vietnam and the Future of the United States Foreign Policy." *The Virginia Quarterly Review* (Winter 1968): 19–42.

Goldman, Eric F. *The Tragedy of Lyndon Johnson.* New York: Alfred A. Knopf, 1969.

Goldwater, Barry. *Where I Stand.* New York: McGraw-Hill, 1964.

Graebner, Norman. *Cold War Diplomacy: American Foreign Policy, 1945–1960.* Princeton, N.J.: D. Van Nostrand Company, 1962.

Hilsman, Roger. *To Move a Nation.* New York: Dell Publishing Company, 1967.

Irish, Marion, and Elke Frank. *U.S. Foreign Policy: Context, Conduct, Content.* New York: Harcourt Brace Jovanovich, 1975.

Jewell, Malcolm E. *Senatorial Politics and Foreign Policy.* Lexington: University of Kentucky Press, 1962.

Johnson, Loch, and James McCormick. "The Making of International Agreements: A Reappraisal of Congressional Involvement." *The Journal of Politics* (May 1978): 468–78.

Johnson, Lyndon B. *The Vantage Point: Perspectives of the Presidency, 1963–1969.* New York: Holt, Rinehart and Winston, 1971.

Kearns, Doris. *Lyndon Johnson and the American Dream*. New York: Harper and Row, 1976.

Kempton, Murray. "Mr. Kennedy's Loyal Opposition." *Spectator*, February 22, 1963, 217–18.

Kennedy, John F. *The Strategy of Peace*. Edited by Allan Nevins. New York: Harper and Brothers, 1960.

Kern, Montague, Patricia Levering, and Ralph Levering. *The Kennedy Crises*. Chapel Hill: University of North Carolina Press, 1983.

Kessel, John. *The Goldwater Coalition: Republican Strategies in 1964*. Indianapolis, Ind.: Bobbs-Merrill Company, 1968.

Kirk, Russell, and James McClellan. *The Political Principles of Robert A. Taft*. New York: Fleet Press Corporation, 1967.

Kolodziej, Edward A. "Congress and Foreign Policy: Through the Looking Glass." *Virginia Quarterly Review* (Winter 1966): 12–27.

Lane, Robert. *Political Ideology*. New York: Free Press of Glencoe, 1962.

Leopold, Richard W. *The Growth of American Foreign Policy*. New York: Alfred A. Knopf, 1964.

Lyon, Peter. *Eisenhower*. Boston: Little, Brown and Company, 1974.

MacNeil, Neil. *Dirksen: Portrait of a Public Man*. Cleveland, Ohio: World Publishing Company, 1970.

Manning, Bayless. "The Americans: 1976." *The Atlantic Community Quarterly* (Summer 1976): 154–71.

———. "Goals, Ideology, and Foreign Policy." *Foreign Affairs* (January 1976): 271–84.

Mayer, George. *The Republican Party 1854–1964*. New York: Oxford University Press, 1964.

Mayer, Karl E. "Surfeit of Diversity." *New Statesman*, February 21, 1964, 278–80.

Morgenthau, Hans J. "The Founding Fathers and Foreign Policy." *Orbis* (Spring 1976): 15–25.

Morse, Wayne. "American Foreign Policy and Vietnam." *North American Review* (September 1967): 6–10.

Nixon, Richard M. *The Real War*. New York: Warner Books, 1980.

———. *RN. The Memoirs of Richard Nixon*. New York: Grosset and Dunlop, 1978.

Olson, William C. "Congressional Competence in Foreign Affairs." *Round Table*. No. 250 (April 1973): 247–58.

Parmet, Herbert. *JFK*. New York: Dial Press, 1983.

Patterson, James T. *Mr. Republican: A Biography of Robert A. Taft*. Boston: Houghton Mifflin Company, 1972.

Peabody, Robert L. "Political Parties: House Republican Leadership." In *American Political Institutions and Public Policy*, edited by Allan P. Sindler. Boston: Little, Brown and Company, 1969.

Persico, Joseph. *The Imperial Rockefeller.* New York: Simon and Schuster, 1982.

Poole, Peter. *The United States and Indochina, from FDR to Nixon.* Hinsdale, Ill.: Dryden Press, 1973.

Raskin, Marcus G., and Bernard Fall, eds. *The Vietnam Reader: Articles and Documents on American Foreign Policy and the Vietnam Crisis.* New York: Vintage Books, 1967.

Roskin, Michael. "From Pearl Harbor to Vietnam: Shifting Generational Paradigms and Foreign Policy." *Political Science Quarterly* (Fall 1974): 563–88.

Rostow, Eugene. "New Challenges to American Foreign Policy, 1963–1968." *Atlantic Community Quarterly* (Spring 1969): 118–24.

Schandler, Herbert Y. *The Unmaking of a President.* Princeton, N.J.: Princeton University Press, 1977.

Schapsmeier, Edward L., and Frederick H. *Dirksen of Illinois.* Urbana: University of Illinois Press, 1985.

Scheele, Henry Z. *Charlie Halleck: A Political Biography.* New York: Exposition Press, 1966.

Schlesinger, Arthur M., Jr. *A Thousand Days.* Boston: Houghton Mifflin Company, 1965.

Sorenson, Theodore C. *Kennedy.* New York: Harper and Row, 1965.

Spanier, John. *American Foreign Policy Since World War II.* 9th ed. New York: Holt, Rinehart and Winston, 1983.

———. *The Truman-MacArthur Controversy and the Korean War.* New York: W. W. Norton and Company, 1965.

Stromberg, Roland N. *Collective Security and American Foreign Policy.* New York: Frederick A. Praeger, 1963.

Taft, Robert A. *A Foreign Policy for Americans.* Garden City, N.Y.: Doubleday and Company, 1951.

Valenti, Jack. *A Very Human President.* New York: W. W. Norton and Company, 1975.

Vandenberg, A. H., Jr., ed. *The Private Papers of Senator Vandenberg.* Boston: Houghton Mifflin Company, 1952.

Waltz, Kenneth. *Foreign Policy and Democratic Politics.* Boston: Little, Brown and Company, 1967.

Watt, D. C. "American Foreign Policy After Vietnam." *The Political Quarterly* (Summer 1973): 271–82.

Westerfield, H. Bradford. *Foreign Policy and Party Politics.* New Haven: Yale University Press, 1955.

———. "Congress and Closed Politics in National Security Affairs." *Orbis* (Fall 1966): 737–53.

White, Theodore H. *The Making of the President 1960.* New York: Atheneum House, 1961.

————. *The Making of the President 1964*. New York: Atheneum Publishers, 1965.

————. *The Making of the President 1968*. New York: Atheneum Publishers, 1969.

Williamsburg, Terry. *The Inmates and Presidential Politics: Prospects for the Future*. Washington, D.C.: Jefferson Publications, 1982.

Wright, Esmond. "Foreign Policy Since Dulles." *Political Quarterly* (April 1962): 114–28.

Zelman, Walter A. *Senate Dissent and the Vietnam War, 1964–1968*. Ann Arbor, Michigan: University Microfilms, 1971.

REPUBLICAN PARTY AND GOVERNMENT DOCUMENTS

Republican Conference of the House of Representatives. *The United States and the War in Vietnam*. Washington, D.C., 1966.

————. *Vietnam: Some Neglected Aspects of the Historical Record*. Washington, D.C., 1965.

Republican National Committee. *Choice for America. Reports of the Republican Coordinating Committee, 1965–1968*. Washington, D.C., 1968.

————. *Official Reports of the Twenty-seventh, Twenty-eighth, and Twenty-ninth Republican National Conventions*. Washington, D.C.

Senate Republican Policy Committee. "The War in Vietnam." Washington, D.C., April 1967.

U.S. Congress, Senate. *A Record of Press Conference Statements for the Joint Senate-House Republican Leadership*. 1961 to 1965 Washington, D.C.

U.S. Congress, Senate. *A Record of Press Conference Statements for the Republican Leadership of the Congress*, 1966 to 1968 Washington, D.C.

U.S. President. *Public Papers of the Presidents of the United States, Lyndon B. Johnson*, 1963–1969. Washington, D.C.

INDEX

Acheson, Dean, 14
Agnew, Spiro, 141
Aiken, George, 37, 61, 106, 119, 125
Arends, Les, 81

Baroody, William, Jr., 112–13
Bay of Pigs, 40
Berlin, 39
Bipartisanship, 7–9, 87, 143, 145, 154
Bliss, Ray, 83–84
Bowles, Chester, 38
Bradley, Omar, 128
Brooke, Edward, 115, 119
Bundy, McGeorge, 69
Burch, Dean, 83
Burgess, Art, 150–53
Bush, George, 130

Castro, Fidel, 29, 40, 43, 46
Chiang Kai-shek, 12, 19
Compact of Fifth Avenue, 30, 63
Congressional Liaison Office, 150
Containment policy, 5, 145
Cooper, John Sherman, 68–69, 125, 131
Cuban Missile Crisis, 45–49, 69
Cuban Resolution, 50

Dewey, Thomas E., 27–28, 60
Diem, Ngo Dinh, 23, 53–55
Dien Bien Phu, 22
Dirksen, Everett M.: background of, 27; on Bay of Pigs, 40; on Berlin, 40; on communism, 45; coordinating committee, role with, 84; Eisenhower, foreign policy under, 31, 37; Fulbright, debate with, 123–24; as GOP's foreign policy spokesman, 146; on Gulf of Tonkin, 68; on JFK's foreign policy, 50; JFK, leadership role under, 35, 144–45; LBJ, support for, 123, 147, 153, 154; *Liberal Papers*, 44; Manila Conference, 108; on Platform Committee, 138; Senate, lacking innovation with, 147–48; Senate Policy Committee Report, disavowal of, 120–21; Ev and Charlie Show, 36; Vietnam, views on, 88, 91, 92, 94, 96, 125
Domino Theory, 20, 59, 88
Dulles, John Foster, 20

Eisenhower, Dwight D.: all-Asian negotiations, 107; campaign of 1952, 17–18; congressional Re-

publicans, relations with, 26–27;
and coordinating committee, 84,
136; Cuba, views on, 40, 48;
and domestic politics, 24; and
domino theory, 59; Goldwater,
possible mission for, 71; and
GOP, revitalization, 144; internationalist wing, leader of, 3;
Joint Leadership, creation of, 36;
Korean War, views on, 17–18;
Korean war negotiations, 140;
LBJ, advice and support for, 89,
99, 128, 152; and Republican
Policy Committee, 25; Vietnam,
break with LBJ on, 134; Vietnam, early views on, 20–24

Findley, Paul, 122
Ford, Gerald R.: chairman of conference, 37, 73; chosen as House
minority leader, 74–75, 78; and
coordinating committee, 84, 87;
on Dirksen, 104, 149; GOP's
response to LBJ's State of the
Union addresses, 98, 113–14; as
House minority leader, 145–47;
on LBJ's leadership style, 78,
149; on Manila Conference, 108;
quarantine of North Vietnam,
96; Vietnam, and GOP's diverse
opinions about, 96; Vietnam,
and House reports about, 80;
Vietnam war, on mismanagement of, 103–4; Vietnam, public
dissent over, 125
Formosa Resolution, 69
Fullbright, J. William: Cuba, critical of Republican response on,
51; Dirksen, debate with, 123–
24; as a domestic critic, 93; Foreign Relations Committee,
chairman, 38; on LBJ's foreign
policy, 100; Nixon, criticism of,

by, 101; and Tonkin Gulf Resolution, 68–69

Gavin, James, 93
Geneva Accord, 22–23
Goldman, Eric, 58, 106
Goldwater, Barry: acceptance
speech at 1964 GOP convention, 66; on Bay of Pigs failure,
41; on Castro, 43; on Cuba, 46;
and foreign affairs, 3; Halleck
and Dirksen, criticism of, 37; on
JFK's foreign policy, 50–51;
Joint Leadership, meeting with,
36; LBJ, criticism of, 72; presidential election campaign
(1964), 61, 63; presidential election defeat, 72–73, 145; Tonkin
Gulf, support for LBJ and, 70;
on Tractors for Freedom, 42; on
Vietnam, 63, 64; Vietnam, opposition to unlimited war in, 90
Goodell, Charles E.: on Dirksen,
76, 82–83, 148–49; as a GOP
leader, 75; GOP's minority
party status, view on, 76; on
Halleck, 76; Halleck, move to
oppose, 74; House white papers,
81; on LBJ, 148–49; loyal opposition, meaning of, 77; on Mel
Laird and GOP reorganization,
77–78; Rockefeller, negotiator
for, 139
Goodpaster, Andrew, 89–90, 134
Griffin, Robert, 74
Gruening, Ernest, 69
Gulf of Tonkin, 67, 79, 100, 116

Haiphong, 96, 106, 121
Halleck, Charles A.: background
of, 27; Bay of Pigs failure, 40;
on Berlin, 39; on communism,
45; JFK, relationship with, 135,

144–45; on JFK's foreign policy, 50; on LBJ's foreign policy, 58, 59; and *Liberal Papers*, 44; as minority leader, 73–74, 147; Show, Ev and Charlie, and, 36–37

Harriman, Averell, 38

Hatfield, Mark, 91, 121

Hilsman, Roger, 33–34

Ho Chi Minh, 19–20, 91, 115

Holt, Pat, 47

Hoover, Herbert, 71

Humphrey, Hubert, 70, 100, 140

Inter-American Treaty, 42

Javits, Jacob, 41, 88, 90, 106, 118–19, 124, 131

Jenner, William, 24

John Birch Society, 68, 84

Johnson, Lyndon B.: Democrats and Republicans, losing support of, 94; on Dirksen, 124; Eisenhower, relationship with, 134; Eisenhower, seeking support of, 89–90; election of 1964, 69–73; GOP, infiltration of, in Senate, 149–53; GOP, response to critics in, 114–15; GOP, use of persuasive powers on, 153; Gulf on Tonkin, 67–69; leadership style, 78; Manila Conference, 108; peace negotiations prior to 1968 election, 140–41; presidency, assumption of, 57–59; Senate Policy Committee Report, response to, 120–21; as a senator, 21; State of Union address (1966), 97; State of Union address (1967), 113–14; Vietnam, using Eisenhower's policies in, 81; Vietnam war, negotiations on, 96; Vietnam war, regulating conduct of, 93

Keating, Kenneth: 46–48, 59

Kennan, George, 5

Kennedy, John F.: Bay of Pigs, 40; Cuban Missile Crisis, 46–49; Halleck and Dirksen, relationship with, 144; presidential election campaign of 1960, 29–31; Republicans, infiltration of, in Senate, 149–50; Republicans, relationship with, 51; travel to Southeast Asia as Congressman, 51; and Vietnamese internal reform, 54

Kennedy, Robert F., 75, 93, 115, 134, 152

Khrushchev, Nikita, 37, 39

Korean War, 12–15, 143–44

Kosygin, Alexei, 127

Kuchel, Thomas, 48, 77, 121, 151

Laird, Melvin: and coordinating committee, 84, 87; described by contemporary, 77; on Dirksen, 119; on Dirksen's reasoning about Vietnam, 149; election of 1964, call for unity after, 73; GOP foreign policy views, support of, 44–45; as a GOP leader, 75, 145; GOP State of the Union Address (1968), 130; on LBJ and the loyal opposition, 76–77; on LBJ's leadership style, 78; South Vietnam, coalition government in, 90; on Tonkin Gulf Resolution, 79; Vietnam, charges LBJ with lack of candor on, 102; Vietnam, on political initiatives with, 81; Vietnam, seeking victory in, 92; Vietnam War, on escalation of, 61

Legislative Reorganization Act of 1946, 9

LeMay, Curtis, 93

Lindsay, John, 89, 138
Lodge, Henry Cabot, 65, 72
Loyal opposition, 8

MacArthur, Douglas, 15
McCarthy, Eugene, 134, 152
McCarthy, Joseph, 16, 24
McNamara, Robert, 64, 89, 93–94
Manatos, Mike, 150–52
Manila Conference, 108
Mansfield, Mike, 148
Mao Tse-Tung, 12
Martin, Joseph, 74
Massive retaliation, 20
Miller, Jack, 138
Missile gap, 30, 39
Morse, F. Bradford, 122
Morse, Wayne, 69
Morton, Thruston, 37, 41, 123–24
Moyers, Bill, 99, 105
Murphy, George, 130

Nixon, Richard M.: all-Asian ne-
    gotiating strategy, 107; on Bay
    of Pigs invasion, 43; and coor-
    dinating committee, 87; and co-
    ordinating committee reports,
    136; Cuba, covert operations
    against, 40; Cuba, on quarantine
    on Soviet arms to, 46; Cuba,
    urges bipartisan support for JFK
    over, 41; Cuban missile crisis,
    support for JFK during, 49; on
    Diem, 55; election campaign of
    1964, role in, 71–72; elections of
    1966, role during, 111–12; on
    Goodell, 75; GOP, charting
    course for, 153; GOP platform
    committee, speech before, 138–
    39; joint leadership, meeting
    with, 36; LBJ, chides for criti-
    cizing GOP, 110–11; as a presi-
    dential candidate in 1960, 29–31;
    as a presidential candidate in
    1968, 133–34, 140–41; secret
    peace plan, refuses details on,
    135–36; as a senator, 16; on
    Tractors for Freedom, 42; as
    vice president, 25, 28; Vietnam,
    claims LBJ prepares for defeat
    in, 60–61; on Vietnam tour,
    106, 117; on Vietnam war strat-
    egy, 92, 99; Vietnam war
    protestors, critical of, 107

O'Brien, Larry, 150
O'Donnell, Kenneth, 151–52

Pearl Harbor, 7, 143
Percy, Charles, 18, 115, 118, 119,
    121
Potsdam Conference, 4
Prendergast, William: 79–80, 82–
    83, 88

Reagan, Ronald, 138–39
Reasoner, Harry, 128
Reed, John, 100
Republicans and the Republican
    Party: conservative wing, 24;
    and containment, 20, coordinat-
    ing committee, creation of, 75;
    and internationalism, 26; as mi-
    nority party under FDR and
    Truman, 6; peace, and prospects
    for, 127–28; as peace party in
    1968, 121; and the postwar pe-
    riod after 1945, 1–10; reorgani-
    zation of party after 1964 defeat,
    74–80, 83–85, 87–88; transitions
    for the party, 143–46; Vietnam,
    division over negotiated settle-
    ment and military victory in,
    131; Vietnam War, philosophi-
    cal support for, 70–71
Rhodes, James, 99

Rhodes, John, 77, 79, 102
Rockefeller, Nelson: and Bay of
    Pigs invasion, 41; on commu-
    nism, 64–65; coordinating com-
    mittee member, 87; during
    election of 1960, 29–30; during
    election of 1964, 61–62; gover-
    nors' resolution, seconding of,
    99; internationalist wing, leader
    of, 3; joint leadership, meeting
    with, 36; Nixon, critical of, 135;
    Nixon, joins forces with, 139;
    presidential race of 1968, entry
    into, 132–33; on Vietnam, dur-
    ing 1964 campaign, 65; Vietnam
    War, plan to end, 133
Romney, George: bombing, urges
    de-escalation of, 122; on bomb-
    ing North Vietnam, 106; con-
    tainment, ineffectiveness of,
    115–16; coordinating committee
    member, 83; governors' resolu-
    tion, refusal to endorse, 91;
    neutralization plan for Vietnam,
    132; as a presidential candidate
    in 1968, 131–32; Soviet
    Union, trip to, 127; Vietnam
    war, calls for congressional de-
    bate on, 99
Roche, Charles, 151
Roosevelt, Franklin D., 5–6, 75–
    76, 114
Rostow, Walt, 151
Rusk, Dean, 78

Schlesinger, Arthur, Jr., 50, 51
Scott, Hugh, 2, 51, 119, 148
Scranton, William, 65
Smith, Margaret Chase, 77,
    118
Sorenson, Theodore, 33–35, 38
Southeast Asia Treaty Organiza-
    tion (SEATO), 22, 52, 79, 90

Sprague, Irvin, 151
Stennis, John, 93
Stevenson, Adlai, 17, 50

Taft, Robert A.: background and
    Senate leadership position, 10–
    11; Eisenhower, disagreement
    with, over Korea, 17; foreign
    policy spokesman, 143,146; iso-
    lationist wing, leader of, 3; role
    during Eisenhower's administra-
    tion,24; Truman, break with,
    13–16
Taftian-Contractural Theory,
    14
Tet Offensive, 131–34
Tower, John, 6, 87, 107, 130–31
Truman, Harry S., 4–7, 12–14,
    16–17, 115

Valenti, Jack, 150–51
Vandenberg, Arthur H.: biparti-
    sanship, formation of, 6–9; bi-
    partisan tradition, 52, 143, 145;
    death, 13; as GOP spokesman
    on foreign affairs, 146; Taft,
    sharing Senate leadership with,
    10–11; vision for future,
    154–55
Versailles Peace Conference, 8,
    111
Vietnam: all-Asian negotiation
    concept, 107; bombing, easing
    of restrictions on, 121–22;
    bombing, increases in North,
    106; civil war during 1940s, 19–
    20; and containment policy, 127;
    under Diem, 53–54; division of,
    under Geneva Accords, 22–23;
    and early post-World War II
    foreign policy, 16, 18–19; as a
    foreign policy issue for U.S.,
    31; French defeat in, 19–23;

House of Representatives reports on, 80–81; and JFK's foreign policy, 51–56; LBJ's goals for, 97; peace negotiations in 1968, 140; troop levels and tactics, 112; U.S. goals for its freedom, 146; and U.S. military strategy, 92–93, 129

Wallace, George, 93
Watson, Marvin, 151
Wilson, Bob, 102, 148
Wilson, Woodrow, 8, 111
World War II, 3–5, 11–12, 18–19

About the Author

TERRY DIETZ is a teacher of American Government at Jefferson High School, Lafayette, Indiana.